Of Cabbages and Kings

Of Cabbages and Kings
And Many Other Things

Marguerite Hurrey Wolf

Illustrations by Shelia Mitchinson

Marguerite Hurrey Wolf

The New England Press
Shelburne, Vermont

The New England Press
P. O. Box 575
Shelburne, Vermont 05482

Library of Congress Catalog Card Number 84-61616
ISBN 0-933050-25-9

*To Tage, in recognition of ten years
of courage among the Wolfs.*

PRINTED IN THE UNITED STATES OF AMERICA

"The Time has come, the Walrus said,
    To talk of many things:
Of shoes—and ships—and sealing wax—
    Of cabbages—and kings—
And why the sea is boiling hot—
    And whether pigs have wings."

from Alice in Wonderland

Contents

In Case We Haven't Met	3
Vernal Vitality	6
Spring Tonic	8
One More Pig Tale	11
Evanescence	15
Black Magic	20
Don't Leave It to Beaver	23
Essence of Spring	26
Vermont Vincit Omnia	31
Remembrance of Sounds Past	34
"And Whether Pigs Have Wings"	38
Fences	42
To Pic or Nic	47
Rites of Passage	53
Even on Sunday in Switzerland	57
The Odd Couple	62
Further Goose Tales	65
Let's Stop for a Sandwich	71
Lord of the Flies	75

This It Not a Recording 78

Fall 81

"And Sealing Wax" 85

More About Men and Women 88

Women's Rites 92

Small World 95

A Wolf in Sheep's Clothing 98

It Was Just One of Those Days 102

"And Ships" 105

"Of Shoes" 110

Trees 115

A Season of Color and Contrast 121

The Christmas Letter 125

Sounds of Winter 129

Winter in Vermont 132

Of Cabbages and Kings

In Case We Haven't Met

If you are familiar with my previous books, you may already know more than you need to know about the Wolf family. But if your library does not include any of these divertisements, perhaps I should tell you what they are about.

My writing is largely concerned with what interests me most, our family and our natural habitat, which by choice and good fortune is northern Vermont. This includes my physician husband George, now officially retired but working full time teaching and consulting, our older daughter Patty, her husband Tage Ström, and their two boys Patrick and Peter, now 8 and 6, our younger daughter Debbie, her husband, Steve Page, and their son Morgan, 3. Our daughters' families do not live under our roof—neither do our sheep, pigs, chickens and turkeys. Patty's family lives in Lille Vaerlose, Denmark, near Copenhagen, and Debbie and Steve live in South Burlington, Vermont, near the University. The two pigs, two sheep, four turkeys, and twenty laying hens are still dependent on us for food and shelter, and they live in or around our old red barn on 17 acres, more or less, of rocky Vermont hillside. The barn also harbors a varying census of uninvited

3

guests, barn swallows (summers only) upstairs, mice, and once a plague of rats, now extinct as of this writing.

We don't miss New York City where we lived for fifteen years. Nor do we miss Weston, Massachusetts, or Mission Hills, Kansas, both beautiful towns, where we were suburbanites for nine years, except for summers which we spent in Vermont. We like living in partnership with the soil and with the four seasons. Of course we moan when the turkeys get out and demonstrate the paucity of their brainpower in finding their way back into their pen. We have been known to smack the solid rump of a pig who knocks the full grain scoop out of our hands when we are aiming at the feeder. And mending old fences or harvesting Vermont's abundant crop of rocks can't really be called recreation. But they are purposeful activities.

A freezer full of lamb chops, hams, chickens and garden produce, and shelves full of pickles and jellies do more for my soul, to say nothing of my body, than a golf trophy. Good thing, because I am not likely to bring home a golf trophy when my score for nine holes approximates what a serious golfer writes down for eighteen.

We like Vermont's five season climate, although I'd prefer an extra May and September instead of the mud season of March and April. We like small things: a small house (in Kansas we lived in a Tudor mansion that had eight bathrooms, a resident ghost, and a cellar fan the size of a wind tunnel), small cars (a Rabbit and a Volkswagon truck), small dinner parties where you don't miss any of the conversation, and especially our three, small, bright and beautiful grandsons.

It seems almost myopic to say that we are contented. Certainly we are not happy about hot and cold running warfare, acid rain from the Midwest falling on our spruce forests, crime and apparent lack of punishment. But when the TV news fades out with its tiny spot of light and the newspapers are bagged up for disposal, we are surrounded by beauty, the perfect roses that George nurtured this year, the flash of a scarlet tanager through the maple tree, the taste of fresh-shelled peas, and the murmuring of the chickens as they settle down for the night. The world is full of a number of soul-satisfying things. Maybe I can't stop mankind from self-destruction. I'd like to safeguard the world for Patrick and Peter and Morgan, but if I can't do that, at least I can share with them the magic of a milkweed pod, the construction of an oriole's nest, or the courage of a snowdrop pushing up through the snow.

Vernal Vitality

How can a snowdrop do it? Towards the end of March when our heavy drifts of crystalized snow recede and the first, tiny snowdrop spears poke up through the icy crust, I welcome them more than a dozen hot-house roses. A few days later their tiny, white bells may again be buried under six inches of sugar snow. I always fear that the fragile-looking blossoms will be squashed. Not at all. Along comes a mellow, sunny day, the snow shrinks down into the earth, and there they are perfectly upright without the least damage from the pressure they've been under. They not only provide the first excitement of long-awaited spring, but they boost my winter-weary outlook on life. In human terms, they show courage under much adversity. The ability to wait quietly and to pause without retreating is rare in our action-oriented world.

If the snowdrop can do that, maybe I can, too! Can I learn to "center down," as the Quakers say, and accept a load without being bent by it?

In the tropics, our snowdrop would be almost invisible among the flamboyant colors of hibiscus, orchids, and anthurium. Even compared to our northern, early-spring flowers, it lacks the heady fragrance of the hyacinth or narcissus. It has neither brilliant color nor perfume to attract bees. In fact the bees are still asleep, and so is most of the flora in the North Country. Only a small chipmunk—his sleek, little, striped body lean from his winter sleep, stuffing his cheeks with sunflower seeds dropped under our birdfeeders—scuttles back into his subterranean labyrinth, brushing against the upright spears and pendulous flowers of the snowdrops. They sway gently, their tiny bells shaken by the touch of his warm fur. A chipmunk who could curl up in a teacup, with only his tail draped over the rim, and three snowdrop blossoms that would hardly fill a teaspoon are mighty enough to assure me that there is always another chance, renewed hope, and another spring.

Spring Tonic

When the crows come out of the woods and the farmers go into them to hang their sap buckets, I am glad that I was born too late for the old rites of spring cleaning and spring tonic. I have seen enough springs to know what a carpet beater looks like and my mother used to reminisce in mid-March about rhubarb and soda, but I was never subjected to those torments. For her the first bright thrust of a crocus and the drip of the icicles at the eaves invoked a tribal memory rather than a current need. Of course I have read about sulphur and molasses, which sound no worse than the oil of the castor bean or the cod's liver which were used in their natural and malodorous state to mortify the flesh in my youth, but I've never tasted sulphur and molasses—and I'm glad of it.

There was, however, a spring ritual our children used to observe when they were growing up in South Burlington. We had a standing offer of an ice-cream cone for the child who spotted the first robin. Of course whoever else was along when we went for the ice-cream cone got one too, but the glory went to the sharp-eyed one. The girls also had a contest to see who could collect the most signs of spring.

When we came back to live year-round in Vermont after an absence of nine years, I found myself looking for these new-old portents. Advertisements for new clothes or car tune-ups don't count. Neither do purple plush rabbits or chocolate Easter eggs. But any natural metamorphosis, even if barely perceptible, does. First, of course, is the lengthening of days, more light which becomes apparent as early as January even though the coldest weather is yet to come. But the additional light at both ends of the day gives us courage to face it. Then there is the occasional thaw with dripping icicles and granulating snowdrifts, even though it is followed by zero weather and the heaviest snowfall of the year. When the ice fishing shanties disappear and a band of open water spreads like a dark shadow across the lake, you can expect the maple trunks to sprout spiles and pails and a crocus to explode into color on the south side of the house.

From then on spring gathers momentum, slowly in our part of the country, but noticeably to the eager observer, even before the snow fences are rolled up at the side of the highway. No one but a Vermonter would call it spring, but there are a few pussy willows, a patch of wild onions near the Winooski River that bears their name, the sharp green of hellebore which quickens the heart more than the lush greens of summer.

The earth steams in the sun and invites the first robins and male red-wings to rest from staking out their territories and come to dinner. It is April before the shad blossoms feather out and a net of green catches in the top branches of the popple trees. The weeping willows give off a golden light long before they blossom or leaf out, and the new growth on the apple trees glows rosy red.

I used to lament the late spring in Vermont, but now I savor it, because, as with many things in life, the anticipation is a large part of the pleasure. There are days when you can see four or five deer grazing with no concern for the traffic along the interstate highway between Bolton and Waterbury. When May finally brings bright, green fields spangled with dande-lions, apple trees in full blossom, and a spill of lilacs at every dooryard, I will have lost count as trillium, wild strawberry, rosy stalks of rhubarb, twin lambs in a meadow, and a wobbly colt are added to my collection.

When Wayne and Ralph Nealy used to let the cows out of their barn in Jericho Center and drive them the two miles to our pasture for the summer, the children and I would go up to watch. Their antics as they sensed the freedom and space after the long winter confinement were predictable but wonderfully entertaining. You can't really say that a cow gambols, prances, or cavorts, but they tried, and their ungainly efforts at lighthearted abandon reduced us to helpless laughter. Who needs sulphur and molasses? Spring itself is the tonic, the best restorative for a winter-weary mood.

One More Pig Tale

I thought we had become wise in the ways of pigs. We have harbored two pigs a year since 1949, except for the nine years we lived in Weston, Massachusetts, and Mission Hills, Kansas, where pigs were not socially acceptable. Our usual *modus operandi* is to buy two six-week-old shoats in May, keep them over the summer, and have them butchered in early November when they are almost seven months old and weigh 200 to 225 pounds. Once, in South Burlington, we kept a sow, had her bred, and welcomed her litter of eleven. It was fun. As it said in the old cigarette ad, they were "so round, so firm, so fully packed." But it was not economical. The fat mama ate several times her weight in pig feed, and the price for the piglets at that time didn't begin to pay for her keep.

We knew how protective a sow is of her offspring. When the vet in South Burlington came to castrate the little boars, he was dismayed to find her in the same pen with the babies. I assured him that she was perfectly gentle and that we often got into the pen to play with the piglets. But we were part of the family and posed no threat. When the vet climbed into the pen, the sow charged and sent him flying over the gate. He

11

landed flat on his face on the barn floor. We had to lure her into a horse stall and close two doors between her and the shoats before the vet could get on with his business.

This year we set off in the truck to a farm in Westford to get two piglets as usual. At the far end of the barn, separated from the main part of the barn by a heavy wooden door, Rudy Botala had the sow in one stall and the five piglets in an adjoining stall. The sow grunted companionably until Rudy grabbed two piglets and started stuffing them into the bags that George and I were holding. Suddenly a rumbling like Mt. St. Helens about to erupt rose to a wild screech of rage, and Mama heaved up on her fat haunches and tried to climb out of her pen. It never occurred to me that she could. But with "Oofs" and a colossal thump, she went right over the top— all 500 pounds of her! Clutching my bagged piglet, I made for the door at top speed. I assumed that Rudy could get her back in the pen. Not wanting her to get out into the main part of the barn, where five milking goats and two kids were penned, I slammed the door behind me and leaned on it with all my strength, feeling that I was doing my part in containing the enraged sow. When something whammed against the other side of the door, assuming that it was the sow, I redoubled my efforts, until I heard George's voice, muffled by the sow's shrieks, "Let me out, for God's sake!" Out he exploded, hugging his pig-in-a-poke, and right behind him, a wild-eyed Rudy whose hand was dripping blood where the sow had bit him.

Not only did they not share my amusement at their frantic faces, George had a few comments that were not too flattering to make about my judgment in cooping them up with a revengeful sow. We paid for the little pigs, loaded them into the cab of the truck with me, and took off with dispatch. Rudy was left to nurse his wounds and make his peace with the

sow, if he could convince her that all danger of further shoat-napping was past.

The piglets wiggled and grunted conversationally on the 15 mile ride home in their plastic bags with holes cut for air and were soon snuffling in the shavings and exploring their new home in our barn. I love to watch baby pigs. They twinkle along on their tiptoes, skitter into a corner, and fix you with a shoe-button eye. But when they lose their initial shyness and allow you to pat them, they are solid and warm.

It's quite true what our dog-addicted neighbors say about us. We are pig people—by preference. It is said perjoratively, but we are flattered by the designation. The fact is that we prefer our pigs to their poodles any day—not in the parlor, of course, but then not all dogs have read *Emily Post* either.

Pigs have been bad-mouthed long enough, "Fascist pigs, male-chauvinist pigs, police pigs, dirty as a pig, fat as a pig, greedy as a pig." Our pigs wouldn't know a fascist from a communist or Chauvin from Barney Miller. They *are* enthusiastic about eating, and they *are* rotund; but they don't bark, growl, sniff, shed, tangle with skunks and porcupines, or bay at the moon. Let's hear it for pigs!

Evanescence

"Nature's first green is gold,
Her hardest hue to hold."

I think of Robert Frost's words each spring when the weeping willows are lucent fountains of gold before they leaf out. They are one of the earliest signs of spring in Vermont. But after the early largesse of daffodils, forsythia, crocuses, and primroses is spent, yellow's complimentary color purple appears everywhere. Johnny-jump-ups poke up bravely between the slates of our walk and turn their little kitten faces to the sun. Striped purple and white and solid purple crocuses follow our smaller yellow ones, and down by the brook tiny violets hide in the new grass. Violets are edible and have a unique flavor, and their leaves are full of vitamin C as well. The candied flowers taste just like the fragrance of sweet violets, but it seems a desecration to eat them. We had a sheep once who preferred flowers to grass and often wandered around with a spray of buttercups dangling from the corner of his mouth. Many flowers are edible. Day lilies are prized in

15

Chinese cooking, and nasturtium blossoms and leaves add the bite of watercress to a salad as well as surprising splashes of color.

Of course some plants are poisonous. Poinsettia and rhubarb leaves, daffodil leaves and bulbs and marsh marigold leaves have caused some unexpected problems. Robert Northrop was fixing himself some scrambled eggs one morning and thought he'd add an onion. So he picked up a bulb and chopped it up into his scrambled eggs. Julia came into the kitchen and grabbed a bite of his concoction.

"Wow! I'd better teach you how to make scrambled eggs. Those are terrible. Where'd you get that onion?"

"There was a bunch of them on top of the front chest."

"Those aren't onions. They're daffodils!"

A couple of hours later Robert didn't feel very well and went upstairs to lie down. A neighbor came in. "What's the matter with Robert?"

"He ate a daffodil, and it made him feel funny."

"Don't you know they are poisonous? We'd better call the Poison Center."

They called both the Center and Donny Miller, their local doctor, who told them to give Robert ipecac, grab a bucket, and start out with both for the emergency room at the hospital in Burlington. All the way in Robert and the bucket were in constant communion. After intravenous feeding and swallows of activated charcoal at the emergency room, Robert was a sadder and wiser man. He was feeling nauseated as well as rather foolish there among cardiac arrests and multiple fractures until he heard the lady behind the curtain in the next booth explain her presence. The end of her finger had been bitten off by a hungry squirrel who mistook it for a nut!

In spite of Jean Kerr's admonition, you CAN eat the daisies

as long as they aren't adorning her dinner table, but please don't eat Jack-in-the-pulpit roots or jewelweed in large amounts.

But let's get back to all the lovely violet and lavender blue that follows the gold rush. The purple-violet of pansies is sensuous opulence to rival gold—royal purple (although I've read that royal purple was really almost crimson and only royal because it was so costly that it was out of the reach of the common man). I love to run my fingers over the pansy petals or rub them against my cheek. Purple iris bloom in every side, front, or back yard. The deep-purple Japanese iris and the small wild ones that admire their reflections in our pool are my special favorites, but some of the huge varieties are far showier and not restricted to purple. They are pink, copper, gold, white, apricot and bi-colored, but the variety found in everyone's back yard in my childhood was lavender. My mother said they faded out after some years and should be dug up, divided, and replanted to restore the color. I don't remember that she ever did it, and the iris in our backyard were always a very pale lavender, the color and scent of my grandmother. She also used Yardley's lavender toilet-water, and when I crush a sprig of lavender blossoms or leaves between my fingers, I can evoke her tiny person, dressed in grey or lavender, with a little lace collar fastened by the cameo brooch I still have.

That's what I always thought grandmothers were supposed to look like, but now that I am one, I don't fit the picture at all. Bare-legged and short-haired, I am not a grandmother. I'm a less limber and well-worn mommy badly in need of pressing! Morgan calls me "Blabby" for reasons he has not divulged and I would rather not dwell on. But he called George "Grandma" for a year! Since he had just started calling us anything at all, being called by any name was just as sweet.

There is another shade of purple that delights me every spring, but it is not in the flower garden. The first thrusts of asparagus are amethyst-tipped spears of jade. They are especially welcome when nothing else is edible inside the garden fence except teen-age radishes or thinnings of lettuce. It is unusual to find purple among the vegetables, with the obvious exception of eggplant's dark satin. Some peas have lavender blossoms, and, of course, there are purple-topped turnips and rutabagas, but not in our garden. No one in our family, except the pigs and sheep, considers turnips, parsnips, or kohlrabi to be food. And I'm not going to plant, hoe, and weed them for the animals when there are enough lettuce and cabbage trimmings, carrot tops, and broccoli leaves to provide barnyard salad. We did grow purple bush beans one year just for fun. They would make a conversation piece except for the fact that by the time your guests see them already cooked they have reverted to their cousin's usual green.

But the explosion of purple at the corner of every white farmhouse in New England and in every side yard or garden from New Jersey to Kansas to Oregon comes in lilac time. They may be French or Persian in origin, but they have become as American as strawberry shortcake and as well-loved. The scent of lilacs evokes memories of Memorial Day parades, high school graduations, and Children's Day at the First Methodist Church in Montclair, New Jersey, when, swathed in Dennison crepe paper thinly disguised as a tulip or a rose, we stumbled through our little pieces, grateful to be partially hidden by the buckets of lilacs footlighting the pulpit.

Alfred Noyes promised that if you "go down to Kew in lilac time you shall wander hand in hand with love." Walt Whitman sang of the nostalgia-provoking fragrance of lilacs in "When

Lilacs Last in the Dooryard Bloom'd." He was mourning the death of Lincoln. Each spring at the edge of cellar holes of abandoned farmhouses in the back hills of Vermont the lilacs bloom and seem to mourn the departed families who enjoyed their fragrance long ago.

The fragrance of lilacs is as evanescent as the end of the rainbow. But the promise of both is that whether or not we are here to smell or see them they will surely come back again.

Black Magic

> I never saw a purple cow,
>   I never hope to see one;
> But I can tell you, anyhow
>   I'd rather see than be one.

> —*Burgess Nonsense Book*

In the same book Gelett Burgess adds,

> Ah, yes! I wrote the "Purple Cow"—
>   I'm sorry, now, I wrote it!
> But I can tell you anyhow,
>   I'll kill you if you quote it!

At the risk of an untimely death, I just did. But inasmuch as Gelett Burgess died in 1951, I don't see the grim reaper over my shoulder. It is such a familiar poem that bars, restaurants, and a gift shop in Boothbay Harbor, Maine, have been named The Purple Cow.

To the best of my knowledge a purple cow has never been observed in Jericho Center. But two years ago I found that no one had ever seen a black woodchuck either.

When I looked out the window and saw a large, coal-black

woodchuck sunning himself on a rock in front of our porch, I couldn't wait to tell George. Of course he didn't believe me, so I set the Hav-A-Hart trap on the rock. And guess what was in the trap the next morning? No, not a purple cow, but the black woodchuck—not just dark brown, but jet black all over. What we don't need in Jericho Center is more woodchucks, so we set out in the truck to relocate him way up the road beyond human habitation. On the way we tried to show him to a couple of neighbors, but nobody seemed to be at home. When we told anyone, which we did frequently the next few days, they suggested that we had trapped a fisher cat, a porcupine, or an oversize mink. There was even mention of pink elephants and purple cows. My credentials as a naturalist are not impressive, but anyone who has lived on a farm in Vermont for many years has a wide acquaintance with woodchucks. I know a woodchuck when I see one, and I don't confuse it with a porcupine or a fisher cat for heaven's sake! After all, he and I had been exchanging glances, nose to nose, through the wires of his cage.

I reassured myself with the notion that if there is albinism in animals as well as in humans, with no pigment, pink eyes, white hair, and pale skin, why couldn't there be melanism, an excess of pigmentation in animals, with black hair, eyes, nose and feet? I found so little interest in my theory that I shoved it back in the dim recesses of my mind, which seem to be getting dimmer at a disturbing rate. I can't dredge up a name or a vital bit of information when I need it, but I can remember the name of the piece of music I tortured at my piano recital in 6th grade, something I don't need or care to remember.

And then on January 9, 1983, Bish Bishop wrote in the Sunday *Free Press* that he had seen a black snowshoe hare in Groton, while on a dead deer count. Now no one would doubt Bish Bishop's word on wildlife, so I phoned him at the *Free Press* for verification. Sure enough, just like my black woodchuck, his snowshoe hare had been totally, unmistakably, black, and he promised to defend my theory if the doubters gave me any more trouble.

Do you suppose the black snowshoe hare turns as pure white in the winter as his peers? If not he would be very visible and vulnerable. Maybe that's why there aren't more of them. Mr. Bishop also said that snowshoe hares and deer are occasionally piebald, like a piebald horse, not just when they are changing their pelage, but mavericks in pigment.

All this seems pretty logical, even to me, but while we are being color conscious, there is one color change in nature which seems like black magic, even though I've heard it explained several times. A ruby-throated hummingbird's ruby throat looks crimson from one angle and black from another. An indigo bunting or a blue grosbeak in dim light appears black. But just let a ray of sunlight fall on either one and you'll gasp at the brilliance of his blueness. The explanation is that the color blue as pigment does not exist in feathers. It is a structural color that is visible only when reflected at certain angles. The red of a cardinal's plumage and the orange and yellow of orioles and evening grosbeaks are pigmented colors. There are chemical compounds (carotenoids) in the feathers. Birds with blue feathers have basal pigment that is dark, but a colorless layer of cells above scatters the light until only blue reaches the eye. I told you it was black magic, but there is a moral to this bit of feathered magic. It is not only beauty that is in the eye of the beholder. There are people whom some people see as dark only because they are seeing them in the wrong light. With a little more light they appear in all the beauty of their true colors.

Don't Leave It to Beaver

Brewer's Dictionary of Phrase and Fable says that old wives' tales are "superstitious stories or beliefs kept alive and spread by credulous old women." While neither Ellen Hensel nor I admits to that description with enthusiasm, the fact is that both of us are in that period misnamed the golden years; and we both take pleasure in believing in the return of spring, the therapy of laughter, and an occasional old wife's tale which turns out to be more fact than fiction. I was not always a believer. During our first years in Vermont, I thought it was silly to fasten little tufts of absorbent cotton on your screen door to keep the flies out, until I realized that we had a plague of indoor flies and my neighbor, who practiced the rite, did not. I just forget to do it now, and besides we have far fewer flies since cows are no longer kept on our land.

When moth balls were suggested as a deterrent to the fragrance of the skunk who settled in for the winter under our porch, I gave it a try. But, either he had an atrophied sense of smell (I would too if I were a skunk) or I didn't use enough, because all that maneuver produced was two pungent aromas instead of one. The skunk did move out, but not until spring, when even a young skunk's fancy turns to thoughts of love.

23

He didn't mind the moth balls a bit. Maybe they kept the moths out of his fur.

The application of dried blood around our vegetable garden in Weston, Massachusetts, separated the cottontails from the carrots, and I subscribed wholeheartedly to that one, until I tried it in Vermont with woodchucks. They either ignored the dried blood or thought it a tasty addition to their salads.

Over the years we've tried more repellents for raccoons than a witch doctor has spells. I can truthfully report that our single-minded, Vermont raccoons savor red pepper on young corn, do not mind the prickle of pumpkin vines on the palms of their paws, enjoy loud music blaring from a radio, and find climbing a fence a midsummer's night's dream for the whole family. The only effective deterrent to raccoons has nothing to do with old wives and a lot to do with electric shock therapy. So far an electric wire strung a few inches above our fence has convinced the raccoons that there is greener corn to be had on the other side of an unwired fence.

But now I am a born-again believer in a tale that is new to this old wife. Where there are ponds there are apt to be beavers, and sometimes the owner's ideas of the uses and abuses of his pond run counter to those of the beavers . Humans like to swim and fish in their ponds. Beavers like to swim, dam, and build condominiums in their ponds.

Ellen and Frank Hensel had a beautiful pond in their woods in Stowe. As soon as a beaver discovered it, his engineering instincts compelled him to improve it to beaver specifications. For a while, Ellen and the beaver swam companionably together, on opposite sides of the pond. Sometimes they changed sides, but it was not a symbiotic relationship. Each night the beaver gnawed down some young "popples" and towed them to his dam site. Each day Frank tore down the night's work.

Now, there is just so much frustration a beaver can take. He began to slap his tail at the first sight of Ellen or Frank, and he bared his strong, yellow teeth so ominously that Ellen found her daily swims were becoming less relaxing, especially after her son-in-law Bruce remarked, "I'm sure glad you don't have a wooden leg!"

Even if the beaver was eager enough to rebuild every night, Frank wearied of the daily demolition. The beaver had to go, and Frank reluctantly shot him. Soon thereafter a second beaver took over. Another son-in-law, Don, told them that he had heard of a sure cure from the Northeast Kingdom. It had worked for Luther Hackett at his vacation home in Elmore. Luther set a galvanized pail upside down on top of a rock at the edge of the pond and placed another rock on top of it. Abracadabra! The very day he set up this cairn his toothy visitor departed. It also works if the pail is set on sticks instead of a rock.

After the Hensels sold their place in Stowe and built a new house in Underhill, a pond was their next project.

One of the first univited but welcome guests was a Canada goose, whose tale you'll find in the chapter called "The Odd Couple." To Ellen's dismay, in April of 1984, she saw a familiar-looking, great-big, flat-tailed, furry fellow busy as you-know-what down at their new pond. When Duncan, Ellen's grandson, came out to spend Easter with Ellen, the beaver had been in residence for a week. Duncan suggested they try the remedy that had worked in Stowe. He set up the upturned pail on a rock, placed the ceremonial rock on it, and, you guessed it, the beaver hasn't been seen since.

If there is a logical explanation, I'm not sure I want to hear it. I'm just enough of an old wife to take it on faith. Nature is full of mysteries, and I like it that way.

Essence of Spring

If someone could distil and blend the delicate fragrances of early spring, it might just lengthen the shelf life of Chanel No. 5 indefinitely. But rather than glamorize the wearer, this scent would evoke in her the remembrance of springs past.

Henry Beston, in *Especially Maine,* wrote that fragrance was the "subtlest of influences, touching the emotion directly. Asking nothing of the mind, it not only wakes in us an emotion of place, but summons up as well a poignant emotion of ourselves as we were in time and the place remembered."

Here in Vermont one of the earliest portents of spring is the fragrant, maple-flavored steam curling up out of the sugar houses. We only tap two trees, so our boiling is done first on the wood stove and then finished off on the electric stove. The delicate essence of maple is there, but it loses something by boiling indoors. Perhaps it is the background smells of wood smoke, wet bark, and decaying leaves. And anyone who has ever sugared cannot taste maple syrup in Chicago or San Francisco without immediately picturing the buckets hanging two or three to each venerable trunk on some remembered sugar bush.

Certain smells that you might not want on your dressing table but that are evocative of early spring are those that, after being frozen all winter, release their essence under the warmth of the sun. The manure on the fields, the various wood scents of the woodpile, the smell of dead grass on the lawn, and the earthy smell of the soggy vegetable garden may not be elegant fragrances, but they symbolize the awakening of the earth from its long winter sleep.

The fragrance of the earliest spring flowers is so delicate and so closely related to the way that they feel to the touch that the senses of touch and smell are fused. Does the soft fur of a pussywillow have a real fragrance? The jade and ivory bells of the snowdrops have no real scent of their own but are somehow suggestive of the smell of the granular snow they are poking up through. Forsythia, shadbush, and bluets have delicate fragrances that hint at the heavier perfumes of late spring to follow when purple and white lilacs exude a halo of fragrance at the corner of every farmhouse, and the gnarled, old, wild apple trees are clouds of pink and white caught briefly among the maples and pines.

I have never smelled skunk cabbage. For years I thought the hellebore down by our pool with its succulent, chartreuse leaves was skunk cabbage, because it came up so early and at the same time. In any event, I'm not in a rush to sniff a plant with such a bad reputation when all the other smells of spring are so pleasantly evocative. On the first, warm, sunny day in April I hang the laundry outdoors instead of tossing it in the dryer so that later, when I bring it in, I can bury my nose in the fresh, sun-scorched scent of the clothes.

The fragrance of grass clippings when the lawn is mowed for the first time immediately reminds me of my childhood. On nice spring evenings we could play outdoors after supper, and up and down the quiet, suburban street you could hear the click-clacking of the hand-pushed lawn mowers as the fathers, who commuted to the city by day, mowed their lawns in the evening. By then tulips and daffodils were in bloom, and the blossoms of the sweet, black cherry tree in the backyard, where I had my treehouse, were falling as silently as snowflakes on the new-mown grass.

Every small child in spring marches proudly with a sticky, brown-stained fistfull of mangled dandelions. Debbie used to pick a handful of purple violets near the brook and stuff them upside down in a glass of water "so I can see their faces looking out while they are swimming."

In early April in Vermont full-flowering spring is a long way off. You can get down on your hands and knees and sniff a crocus or pick a handful of chives that are already up and add their oniony bite to some cottage cheese. You can smell the wet bark of the pine trees and breathe in the earthy leaf-mold scent of the flower gardens as you release a few daffodil leaf spikes from the rotting leaves they have impaled on their way up. These are portents and promises that lift the heart, but you have to wait for several weeks for the fulfillment of those promises, when the air is alive with the humming of bees and the apple blossoms, hyacinths, lilacs and sweet violets perfume the air. The best parfums de Paris are made from real flowers, acres of them grown in southern France 'til just before their peak. No wonder their distillate is so expensive. A truckload of blossoms may produce an ounce or less of perfume. And in spite of the labor and expense, very few perfumes capture the precise scent of a rose or a freesia. Coty does very well with Lily of the Valley, but I have never smelled a perfume that evoked the heavy rich scent of gardenia.

Perhaps the senses cannot be separated arbitrarily. You need to hear the hum of the bees, see the pink buds and white flower petals of apple blossoms, and feel their cool satin texture to experience the fragrance of apple blossoms. Its the whole sensory experience that quickens your pulse and lifts your spirits and makes you glad that you are alive and in Vermont in Spring.

Vermont Vincit Omnia

The reason so many ethnic jokes cause resentment is that the humor is based on the assumption that some derogatory characteristic is typical of the entire nationality or race. Such generalizations as Swedes are dumb, Poles are dirty, Italians are gangsters, and Mexicans are procrastinators are guaranteed to offend anyone with roots in one of those countries.

Vermont humor, on the other hand, gives the common man the last word. It is based on the age-old idea of the stuffed shirt with the top hat slipping on a banana peel. Lo, how the mighty (the pompous city slicker) has fallen! But it isn't a banana peel that causes the city slicker's downfall in Vermont humor. It is the understated, quick wit of the Vermonter that pricks the balloon. He may be sitting on a country store porch or pausing at the end of a harrowed row when answering the tourist's question. He is the same chap who, according to the city folk, subsists on a diet of tobacco juice and timothy stems.

Vermonters especially enjoy Vermont humor because, as Ralph Nading Hill pointed out in a panel on Vermont humor, the Vermonter always comes out on top.

When the smart-mouthed salesman asks the Vermont store-keeper to make change for an eighteen dollar bill, the store-keeper looks him straight in the eye and says, "Yes, would you like three sixes or two nines?"

Then there was the owner of a hardware store in the Northeast Kingdom. It was not a busy store, just a few paying customers a day or a neighbor stopping in to visit by the stove at the back of the store. One day a man who had recently moved to Vermont from Boston came in and demanded half a length of stovepipe. The storekeeper ambled to the back of the store and told his visiting neighbor, "That durn fool out there comes in and asks for a half a length of stovepipe." Then, noticing out of the corner of his eye that the customer had followed him, he recovered smoothly adding, "And this fine gentleman wants to buy the other half!"

Walter Hard was a master at remembering these homely anecdotes and building a poem around each one. All of his poems are about the neighbors of his childhood and early years in Manchester, Vermont.

Jake was just such a character. He had been a grave digger for several years when his boss told him he was getting "too all-fired slack" and digging the graves too shallow. "Jake pulled the end of his handlebar moustache. 'Ain't heered of anybody gittin' out of 'em hev yu?'"

Every collector of Vermont humor has a story about a tourist who has lost his way and the Vermonter who prides himself on giving directions politely and accurately but bafflingly to the tourist.

Walter Hard tells one about a woman with dark glasses who called out from the driver's seat, "Are you acquainted hereabouts?" Nate, whose family had farmed these acres for several generations, was affronted enough to require a space of time before answering. She said she wanted to go to Turner's Cove. Nate pointed down the road and said, "You jest keep goin' down the rud 'bout two miles. Thar's a new concrete bridge there. Wal, t' get t' the Cove you turn off 'bout half a mile this side that bridge."

Tourists frequently ask how many pigs, sheep, and cows you have in the same way that an elderly spinster, at a loss as to what to say to your children, invariably asks how old they are and in what grade in school. One day Miss Cole was asked, "How many chickens in that brood?" Without looking up she said, "Twelve. Then thar's two that runs around so fast I can't count 'em."

Carl Carmer wrote, "Dwell among the Vermont hills and valleys for a decade and, while you are still regarded as a foreigner by your neighbors, your friends from another day and place will already observe the beginnings of an inevitable victory . . . Vermont vincit omnia."

I know we have changed. I resent any implication that someone who lives in the country is dull-witted. You not only have to be able-bodied to live independently in the country, you have to be able to use every small skill you rapidly acquire and call upon your wits, when you strength or skill is lacking. Our academic degrees have never rocked us out of a ditch or driven a fence post into inhospitable soil. And my fifteen years in New York City taught me nothing about igniting fireproof wood, plucking a chicken, loading a pig, or keeping raccoons on the outside of our garden fence. But my immersion in Vermont has shown me how funny I have been in all of these roles and how especially ridiculous the city slicker is when he slips on the banana peel of his pseudo-superiority.

Remembrance of Sounds Past

Recently I heard Ed Asner say on TV, "The sound of that school bell goes right through me just like it did years ago." Suddenly I remembered the jangle of the school bell in elementary school. My classmates and I had an irrational fear of being late in grade school. The sin was called "tardy," and it was shameful. Times absent and times tardy went on your report card. You'd far rather be marked absent, but if you weren't in your classroom when that bell on the outside wall of the school clanged, you might as well wear a red "T" blazoned on your sweater. Could that be why I am almost always on time now? Some children must have been late. We all walked to school. It was over a mile, and we not only walked to and from school, we walked home for lunch and back—more than five miles a day total. It never occurred to us that a parent might take us to school. My father bought his first car, a Studebaker touring car, when I was ten. He was the only one who drove it and then only on Sunday to Sunday school and church and for a ride in the afternoon.

There were other school sounds that I haven't heard for years. Do children still compete for the dubious honor of thumping out the chalk dust from the erasers on the school steps? And the clock in each classroom made a loud click as it measured off each minute. How long those minutes were, although I don't remember disliking school. It was just there, and I was just there in it. The years are interminable in childhood, a time when your next birthday is an achievement rather than a knell.

This stream of consciousness carried me further to sounds from my childhood that our own grown children would not even recognize. When you lifted the "receiver" of the telephone, a crisp voice said, "Number pleeuz." That was "central," and you called her central not operator. You told her the number you wanted, and she rang it for you. Dialing was unknown, and every phone came in one color—black. The phone had two pieces, a receiver and an upright mouthpiece in the shape of a foot-high daffodil.

If you woke in the very early morning, you could hear the milkman's horses' hooves clop, clopping along the street. The horse seemed to know the stops, because he would pause, the milkman would jump down with his rattling, laden basket, and the horse would go on without him, slowly, to the next customer's house. My room was at the back of the house, and I could hear the milkman's footsteps on the walk around the side of the house. I then heard the thud of bottles—yes, glass bottles with cardboard tops—as he set them on the back steps.

Later in the day there was the sound of another delivery, the iceman. He would come and take a look in your wooden icebox and then go back to his open truck where the ice was covered by a tarpaulin to get the proper-sized chunk. You'd hear him chipping it down to size and then the great thud when he dropped it into the ice chest. You could also hear the drip, drip of the melted ice water into the flat pan under the icebox.

Remember the mailman's whistle? Mr. Selleck walked from the post office on Bloomfield Avenue, crisscrossing the length of Midland Avenue, all the way to the boundry between Montclair and Upper Montclair twice a day! He came at 10:00 a.m. and then again at 2:00 p.m., and he blew his whistle at intervals as he made his way up the street. He carried the mail in a large, brown, leather shoulder bag. They still use those in some towns, but mercifully mail order houses were few and so were magazines and junk mail.

We never heard a snowmobile, a juke box, or a video game. Our first radio was a crystal set. You had to maneuver the little finder around on the crystal to find the station, and then only one person could listen to the Happiness Boys or Eddie Cantor with earphones unless you divided the apparatus and made two earpieces out of it.

If we heard an airplane, it was such a novelty that we ran outdoors to see it. Then we'd see a biplane with a pilot who wore a leather helmet and goggles just like Snoopy playing the Red Baron. I was twelve when Lindbergh crossed the Atlantic, and we heard the newsboys shouting "Extra! Extra! Lucky Lindy reaches Paris!"

We didn't hear the crash of Wall Street, but we felt it. The father of one of my friends lost his job, and men who used to go to offices were selling apples and pencils on the streets of New York. It didn't seem possible in our comfortable suburb where we believed that everything was getting bigger and better and where the World War to end wars had made the world safe for democracy only ten years before.

What sounds will our three little grandsons remember from their childhood? Will they be electronic games, jets, and racing cars? They have parents who are attuned to nature, so I hope they will also remember the baa of a lamb, a hermit thrush's liquid melody at dusk, and the chorus of peepers in the spring. There is no generation gap in these sounds. They were here before atom bombs, and if man stops mucking around with nature, they will be here forever.

"And Whether Pigs Have Wings"

Halos, maybe. Wings, no. Over a period of twenty-five years we have been on a first name basis with sixty-one pigs, which would be a lot of pigs if they were all in residence at the same time. Remember the commotion that pigs en masse caused in Stowe in 1982? A single pig, Miss Piggy, for instance, or Charlotte's pen pal in E. B. White's story, is treated with respect, but multiple pigs have been second-rate citizens ever since Circe turned Ulysses' companions into swine.

Following Noah's example, our census both in the house and in the barn goes two by two. If you are going to have one of something, you ought to have two for companionship—two pigs, two sheep, and two geese. Of course you have to have more than two chickens unless you are on a very low cholesterol diet. We have twenty-four laying hens. We don't keep pairs for procreation, so often they are both female. Who wants a boar or a ram around the place unless you are in the breeding business? We raise our animals for home consumption, and a full grown male is not likely to be toothsome. He is also more than likely to be aggressive, and I don't like to be pushed around by a creature bigger and far stronger than I.

Because I have been locally referred to as "the pig lady," I find that I am considered an expert on porcine matters. I'm not. My dubious renown springs only from the fact that I wrote a story about our trials and errors in learning how to load a pig. It is true that I'd rather have two pigs in the barn than one dog in the house, which makes me suspect among my neighbors. I don't hate dogs. It is just that I don't think any animal belongs indoors. Parents, children, and grandchildren can cause enough confusion without adding barking, sniffing, muddy paws, and dog hair to the menage.

Pigs are friendly, dedicated, entertaining, and the most efficient producer on a small farm. But I am surprised to find how many people are disgusted or frightened by them. "Will they bite?" is the usual nervous question from my guest, rural or urban. They never have, and I've been in and out of the pens for years. When George cleans the pen he pushes them around. They do love to bite the shovel and shove the shoveller, but he has never been nipped. I would hesitate to tangle with a sow and her litter if she didn't know me, but most new mothers are equally protective. Another myth is the idea that a pig's tail curls in one direction in the northern hemisphere and the opposite way south of the equator. I've never raised pigs in Peru, but it seems highly unlikely.

Joan Cross, our neighbor who animal-sits for us if we are away, insists that one of our pigs bit her, but I am equally firm in my opinion that the pig thought she was offering something to eat in her hand and nibbled experimentally.

We once had a goat, and once was more than enough, though I know that goat lovers will rise up in their defense. Once when I was giving a talk, I referred to our goat as "foolish," and two members of the audience objected vociferously. But myths about goats are even more widespread than

39

fear of pigs. It is commonly believed that goats eat everything including tin cans. Nonsense! A goat's narrow jaw couldn't get around a can. Nor do they eat mittens, tires, or golf balls. They will eat some plants that sheep eschew, and they are curious about everything and will mouth unfamiliar objects. Our goat delighted in pulling freshly-washed clothes off the line, nipping a garden glove off your hand, or tugging at your pant leg, but the soggy evidence was always to be found at the scene of the crime.

Because we have lived in the country and kept animals, we have been asked questions that would have surprised me as a city dweller. An obstetrician, of all people, asked George what caused lactation in the cows that shared our pastures. He apparently made no connection between the bovine process and that by which he earned his living.

But our chickens provoke the oddest questions. Another doctor asked George in all seriousness how the rooster could get the sperm through the hard shell of an egg to fertilize it without breaking it. Now that is not too strange, if you consider that most people have not seen an egg until it is either sitting in the nest or in a container at the supermarket. Most of my own early knowledge of anatomy came from watching the butcher dress off a fowl and expose a whole graduating series of golden yokes. But chickens are all pre-eviscerated now, and a child of today has probably never seen the interesting contents of a crop or a gizzard.

"Where is your rooster?" we are frequently asked, and when we say that we don't have one, the usual response is an incredulous, "Then how can you have eggs?" If you reply that women ovulate regularly, they are dumbfounded and mutter, "Yes, but that's not EGGS!" They have never seen a human egg. Neither have I, but a hen's egg for them wouldn't exist unless it had been fertilized.

When I told a friend that I was going to grow French horticultural beans she exclaimed, "Oh, you mean they'll be already split down the middle?" Until I went to California I had never seen globe artichokes growing, but I am surprised how many people have never picked peas from the vines or dug up a potato plant.

Most of our out-of-state guests come in the summer, and several of them have asked if they can help make maple syrup while they are here. Apparently you just plug into the maple tree any old time of the year and turn on the spigot. To compensate for this disappointment, some Vermont towns keep snow in the freezer so they can put on a sugar-on-snow party in August with the syrup that had been boiled down in March.

The misconception that regaled our children the most happened long ago when they were only four and six but already wise in the ways of the barnyard, even though we only spent our summers in Jericho. Friends of ours from New York Hospital stopped by one summer day with their two little boys and two elderly aunts. One of the ladies announced that she was a birder. She admired our resident phoebe and the delegation of barn swallows twittering on the telephone wire and the redwings creaking in the cattails. She wandered down to the brook through the meadow where Wayne Nealy had previously pastured his cows. She returned proudly clasping a rather dry brown circle the size of a plate. "Look at this unusual bird's nest! I can't wait to find out what bird makes its nest on the ground in your field. Do you suppose it was a cowbird?" Wide-eyed, our two little girls stared open-mouthed and then collapsed giggling on the ground. They could hardly wait till she left to shout, "It was a meadow muffin!"

Fences

Before I built a wall I'd ask to know.
What I was walling in or walling out.
Robert Frost

"Something there is that doesn't love a wall," Robert Frost muses at the beginning of his poem "Mending Walls." Yet he and his neighbor mended the stone wall that divided their property each year—not to keep Frost's apple trees out of the other man's pine woods or the pine seedlings from squeezing through the holes to steal Frost's apples—but simply because "Good fences make good neighbors."

An English friend was troubled by our open suburban lawns and gardens. Most gardens in an English suburb are walled. An enclosed garden becomes an additional room in summer. It is private, and the walls are used as backdrops for charming flower arrangements as well as for climbing vines and espaliered fruit trees. That is walling-in rather than walling-out, making an enclosure that belongs to the family. Are the English more private than we are, or is it simply that for a long time there was so much space in this country that it did not have to be

walled in? In the countryside where we live walls are functional rather than decorative. They are for keeping our cows, sheep, and geese inside the fence, or in the case of our vegetable garden, for keeping the rabbits, deer, woodchucks, and raccoons out.

Stone walls, like the kind Robert Frost was mending, started out to be doubly useful. In Vermont you have to do SOMETHING with the annual crop of rocks that the frost heaves up out of the earth. And you need to enclose your fields to protect your corn from peripatetic cattle or to keep your own cows from becoming peripatetic. The stone walls in Ireland are triple-purpose. They keep the sheep in, mark jealously guarded boundries, and provide a more suitable resting place for the everlasting stones.

Cemeteries are fenced, but has any one of its residents ever tried to get out, or is there any reason why someone should not get in? The gate is usually open anyway, so the fence is more a delineation to show respect for an area reserved for the dead.

Tom Sawyer's fence was a status symbol. Fences must be painted and kept in good repair to show that you are just as responsible as your neighbor.

Some walls tell a sad story. The Wailing Walls in Jerusalem, said to be a remnant of the Temple of Herod which was destroyed in the first century A.D., became a gathering spot each Friday for lamentations for the Dispersion and the lost glories of Israel. But the saddest wall and great shame of modern history is the fortified wall in Berlin, severing a homogeneous city, a monument to the stupidity of war.

The Great Wall of China—standing 25 feet tall and 15-30 feet wide, winding some 1500 miles through the countryside and mountains, and consuming the labor and lives of thou-

44

sands—was built to protect China from the northern bar-barians. Many invasions proved that it had little military utility, but it serves not only as an impressive tourist attraction but also as an awesome architectural achievement.

When we lived in Kansas City, we had a wealthy neighbor who lived behind high brick walls. There was an ornate, locked, iron gate and an electronic eye at the entrance to the drive-way. When you rang the bell at the gate, you were observed from the house and either the gate was swung open or you were ignored. If you wanted to plead for admittance, there was a phone box at the gate for that purpose. Somehow I never had the urge to run over to the K's to borrow a cup of sugar.

Although it was an affluent neighborhood (our house had been given to the Endowment Association of the University of Kansas and went with George's job), no one else lived in a fortress. In fact, the few ostentatious families wanted you to see their replicas of Greek sculptures in their Italian gardens. It did give me pause one evening to see an elephant, complete with decorated howdah, being led up the long curved driveway to another house. It wasn't a pink elephant! It was your everyday, weathered, grey, zoo variety, and in the howdah were two laughing ladies in evening dress. It seems the hosts were giving a benefit for the renowned Nelson Art Gallery. The guests had the choice of driving to the door in their cars or parking on the street and taking the elephant. Kansas City was full of surprises.

There are some fences that combine walling in or walling out with classic beauty. The horse farms in Kentucky, where a dignified, pillared, white mansion right out of *Gone With the Wind* is surrounded by rolling, green fields enclosed with white fencing, are repeated with equal charm in north-central

45

Florida. When Thomas Jefferson designed the University of Virginia and Monticello, his fondness for curves in architecture inspired him to build the undulating serpentine walls in Charlottesville.

The hedgerows of the English countryside and the lilac hedges in Denmark are a natural fencing. Have you tried to get through a thorny hedgerow in England? And they are a fragrant as well as a visual delight. In Ireland I begged George to stop the car so that I could see close up that those hedges were really fuchsia and rhododendron. They were. And the poinsettia hedge at my cousin's home in Honolulu looked like a florist's shop on December 24th.

Isn't it a shame that the wall in Berlin is an ugly, fortified, negation of freedom instead of a linden-lined footpath where the families that are now separated by this barrier could stroll together on a Sunday afternoon?

To Pic or Nic

Samuel de Champlain probably was the first white man to picnic on the shores of the lake that bears his name, but to the Indians there was no other way of eating in the summer. There are a lot of white squaws lurking in the Green Mountains, because the word picnic sends most of us into a skirmish of eager preparation and some, including my husband, into a mild depression.

Although an ardent nature lover in-between meals, when lunch is ready George prefers it indoors where the ice supply is handy, the stove smoke-free, and the chairs more tenderly disposed to his nether regions than logs or rocks.

He has been known to mention the usefulness of screens in keeping people and flies segregated. He does not relish an ant on his deviled egg, sand in his hamburger or salt left at home on the kitchen counter. Neither do I, but I consider them calculated risks rather than catastrophes, and the more I calculate, the less the risk.

I suppose the reason so many women and children favor picnics over indoor meals is that it is infinitely more carefree and relaxing to watch the contents of a tuna fish "samwich" spill on the ground rather than on the dining room rug. From the children's point of view, a meal tastes better without admonitions about the distance of cups from the edge of the table, the esthetics of chewing behind sealed lips, and the desirability of remaining immobile from chicken noodle soup to junket.

In fact, mobility is one of the great assets of picnics. It allows the loner to ruminate on a rock above the waterfall, and the generations to gap happily according to their wonts. Children, puppies, and kittens enjoy tangling and rolling in clutches. Most so-called adults favor leg and elbow room within conversational but not collision distance of each other.

So I forego some borderline picnic possibilities, and George humors me by eating in the wild a few times each season. To my amazement he even agreed to a picnic under the huge Douglas fir trees on our Kansas City lawn one May, when there was a solid carpet of violets—purple, deep red, pale blue and white—completely enclosed by a curtain of branch tips that hung almost to the ground. Of course we squashed the violets we sat on, but the luxury of having violets enough to squash was part of the pleasure. Twenty feet away, beyond the hedge, cars were zooming up the hill. In our dim, fragrant bower, a unicorn nibbling a pale violet would have looked more at home than George and I, cross-legged, nibbling dill pickles and ham sandwiches. That picnic was a success, but I never pressed my luck in suggesting that we repeat it.

I must admit though that some of our picnics have been less romantic. One real disaster was shared with Sam and Jane Rowley, with whom we have shared many soon and never to be forgotten moments over the past thirty-five years. It happened long ago before our children and theirs became civilized. They were visiting us in Jericho, with their three children,

Dunham, Sharon, and Peter. With our Patty and Debbie, that meant five children between the ages of three and eight. We were an odd, but not unwieldy number, except when we overstuffed our new army Jeep. There were two seats in front and the small open tonneau in the rear for nine people, thermos jugs, assorted-sized bags of food, towels, bathing suits, sweaters and at least one favorite object per person. These ranged from Sam's snorkel to three-year-old Peter's "plow," a defeated-looking pillow without which he could not draw a happy breath but could manage to scream his head and our ears off.

The Jeep opened up new fields for us. It could sashay up ferny lumber roads, ford rocky streams, and ride unscathed over granite outcroppings that would disembowel a conventional car. Occasionally one of the newly opened fields would resent our intrusion and retaliate with an instant swamp or huge hidden boulder that would lift the Jeep right off the ground, suspending it sputtering in frustration, wheels still spinning uselessly.

But this day George and Sam had studied a geodetic survey map and decided to follow a lumber road to a stream hitherto unexplored by us. The weather looked ominous, but the thought of the day indoors with the young sent us over the sides into the Jeep. The lumber road must have been abandoned for a long time. It was much rockier, overgrown, and longer than we had anticipated. Sam and George rode up front on the two cushioned seats and gloried in the challenge of adventure, but Jane and I and the five kids wedged in back on the bare floor, bouncing up, slamming down, and ricocheting with each impact, were developing saddle sores with no saddles. Suddenly the road stopped and so did we—so suddenly that enough heads knocked together and enough toes got squashed to make the hills resound with the banshee wails of

49

the children. We untwisted ourselves and fell over the sides in eager quest of the brook. A thin trickle wound its unenthusiastic way through the center of a dry, rocky stream bed. But though the brook was almost dry, nothing else was. The mossy ground squished, the trees seemed to drip, and the wood we gathered was so wet that it produced only enough smoke to frustrate our small firemakers but not enough to discourage the clouds of black flies and gnats who spread the news of our picnic far and wide. While Sam blew himself dyspneic trying to encourage the tiny flame, the kids each found a stick for impaling hotdogs and each other. They suspended the hotdogs hopefully over the tiny flicker that looked like Tinkerbell in extremis, just before she was revived by the faith of her young audience. Just as the fire was beginning to hiss enough to steam the underside of the hotdogs, there was a crash of thunder, and before we could dismember the rolls, the skies opened and sluiced down. The children hovered over the wilting fire, jabbing their hotdogs into its smoky remains. A bright flash of lightning illuminated the circle. Peter, afraid of lightning, ran screaming to Jane. Dunham protested that his "hotdoggy" fell in the fire. Debbie squatted on the ground sucking her thumb and as much of her foot as she could twist in the vicinity of her ear. Their T-shirts clung to their wet torsos, and rain dripped off their noses. We gathered the soggy remains of food and children and boosted them into the Jeep that now had about a half-inch of water in the back.

We bounced and jostled home through the storm, Peter still screeching at every flash of lightning, Sharon and Debbie snuffling softly, and Dunham, still holding his stick, protesting the loss of his "hotdoggy." Shivering and hungry, those who weren't crying began to snicker and guffaw. Finally, we were all laughing hysterically, with tears, rain, and blood from black

50

fly bites coursing down our faces. A picnic to remember. All the children are married now with children of their own: Patty in Denmark, Sharon in Chicago, Debbie in Vermont, Peter, who gave up his "plow" and his fear of lightning quite a while before he became six feet tall, and Dunham, with the Peace Corps in Africa, and now in Putney, Vermont, teaching other emissaries to foreign countries.

There was another picnic with Thorn and Muriel Holder and their boys, Tim and Kit, at a beautiful state park in Maine. The weather was perfect—gentian sky, piquant breeze, warm sun. We carried the food to a table in a grove of pine and birch. The kids went off swimming, and Thorn poured us a libation which he had discreetly put in a thermos bottle that morning. The sun and rocks warmed us above and below, and the balsam, red clover, and milkweed were fragrant. Suddenly, a state park ranger had joined us.

"Have a GOOD time folks," he said, pointing to our thermos. "I'm sure that's just orange juice you have there, because you and I both know that liquor is not allowed in this park, and you look like law-abiding citizens."

He strolled away, smiling and whistling and glancing back while we gazed into the depths of our paper cups at a brew not quite so sweet as it had seemed moments before.

The most exciting picnics in my childhood were the ones that combusted spontaneously. We would be playing in someone's yard when suddenly the thought of eating in the tree house in my cherry tree or in a cave that we had discovered in the woods would send us quivering into the nearest kitchen to rustle up provender and parental permission.

What is this aura that illuminates a picnic? It is some kind of sharing of food and drink and companionship in a wild and beautiful setting that goes back as far as "A jug of wine,

51

a loaf of bread and thou beside me singing in the wilderness." The wilderness, still readily available in Vermont, and our inherited need for rapport with it are as important as the bread and wine, but the *thou* gives it special meaning. You see, I am an incurable romantic, but things keep happening that make me that way. When George and I were married, my father gave us one hundred dollars for a honeymoon. And it lasted us ten days! We lived simply, but any other way would not have occurred to us. We rode rented bikes, carrying our lunch in the baskets on the handlebars. I was very conscious and proud of my new wedding ring. I would have liked George to have one too, but he showed no enthusiasm for a ring, and our budget was very tight. One summer, thirty-one years later, George and I returned to the same village. We had never been back in the meantime, and we were delighted to find it so unspoiled and the countryside still deserted. We rented bicycles again and rode out to our old haunts. Wild roses and bayberries scented the soft breeze. Everything was the same except my leg muscles. On one long hill, even after standing up on the pedals and exerting myself as much as I could, I had to get off and push the bike. George waited for me at the top of the hill. When I puffed up alongside, he said, "Look what I just found here in the grass at the side of the road." In his hand was a man's gold wedding ring. He tried it on. It seemed to stick for a moment and then slipped over his knuckle, fitting perfectly on the third finger of his left hand. He wore it for a long while, until it wouldn't fit over an arthritic knuckle, as a pledge of faith, not necessarily in picnics, but in what picnics or marriage are all about—sharing—blisters or bread, it really doesn't matter.

Rites of Passage

Can you remember when everyone dressed up to go travelling? When I was small and went by train from New York to Oregon or by boat from Hoboken to Cherbourg, my sister and I had "travelling dresses," navy blue (practical) pussy-willow silk (washable), sailor hats with elastic under the chin, and white cotton gloves that we wore night and day. That was so that when we were allowed to take them off to eat, a minium of soot and unfriendly bacteria would get into our mouths.

The dining car was a sparkling, tinkling, source of haute cuisine, with starched-linen napkins the size of tablecloths, which had very little staying power in small laps. It was a study in black and white—the black leather chairs, the white tablecloths, and the white jackets on the black waiters. Everything was cooked in the train's galley and arrived on plates so hot that you touched them with awe and trepidation. "Fast" applied to the service not the food,

When I was seven, we went to Europe on the Olympic, my parents, my grandparents, my sister and I. Again, travel was treated as a formal adventure, worthy of rites of passage. Friends sent flowers and fruit baskets to the boat. Other friends came to see you off, and once again you dressed for the occasion. With my teetotaler parents there was no champagne or even wine, but it was still a gala event, even if you travelled second class.

No one had imagined going to Europe by plane. It would be another five years before Lindbergh's feat caused all the New York morning papers to put out an afternoon extra.

My own first flight was a momentous occasion. It was before we were married. George and I, having had summer jobs in the Adirondacks and then a visit with my parents in Maine, decided we could save enough money to fly from Boston to Newark by hitchhiking to Boston. That was in 1938. The plane was not a jet. Stewardesses were required to be nurses, and they were pretty and eager to please. The Newark airport was so small that we climbed down out of the plane, took a shortcut across a field, jumped over a fence, and hailed a bus to Montclair.

Last fall at the Orlando airport we disembarked through one of those accordion tubes that attach to the plane like a vacuum cleaner, walked a mile or two through corridors, got on an elevated shuttle subway that transported us to the main airport while a disembodied voice welcomed us to Orlando. But somehow travelling isn't that much fun anymore. Your under-the-seat bag won't quite squeeze under the window seat. The seat belt has just been embracing a midget, which reminds you that you are thickening in the waist. The little overhead ventilator is aimed at your ear. You can't understand what the captain is saying. The man behind you sneezes, coughs, and blows his nose from take-off to landing, and your drinks are served in styrofoam cups which are even worse than plastic ones. I think styrofoam is also the main ingredient in your lunch.

54

I have been told that the pre-packed meals now served on transcontinental Amtrack trains look like airplane meals but taste better. Does something happen to your taste buds at 32,000 feet, or does the altitude affect the food in spite of the pressurization? But the function of food on the plane is principally busy work to alleviate the boredom. It takes three minutes to pry off the tops of tiny salad dressing or cream containers without spraying their contents over your neighbor on the left. The vegetable is always carrots and is always caramelized. The meat cuts easily but is unidentifiable. It could be filet mignon or wild horse but probably is neither.

It never occurs to me that the plane might crash, though I have often been seated near some woman who nervously voices the opinion that it will. What would be so terrible about dying in a plane crash anyway? Given the choice I'd prefer it to cancer or stroke any day.

If I take off my shoes, they shrink and can hardly be coaxed back on my feet. Don't explain to me about oedema. You forget I am married to a doctor. I suppose you don't think the cleaners shrink clothes after the Christmas holidays either.

If they can develop planes that go as fast as the Concorde, why are the planes stacked up fifteen in a row waiting for take-off for half an hour with all the engines burning up hundreds of gallons of fuel?

In spite of my husband's remark that I'd be happier in the Stone Age, I really don't want to cross the plains in a covered wagon. And I don't miss those childhood train trips from Montclair to Hoboken, seated on those abrasive plush seats, with my feet stuck straight out in front of me. I can still smell that mixture of coal smoke, stale cigars, and chewing gum. No wonder I was prone to car sickness whether I was riding backwards or forwards.

What I do miss is the little attentions, the spotless ocean liners smelling only of paint and canvas, or the drama of a sleeping berth being made up by a smiling porter, and the tender, loving care of the stewardesses when flying was a novelty.

Where did the excitement go? No one watches the stewardess as she drones through her spiel about the oxygen mask, except a little old lady on her first flight, or my small grandsons, Patrick and Peter who watch everything with interest in spite of the fact that they have flown the Atlantic many times.

No one is in awe of the fact that we are flying at 32,000 feet at 500 miles per hour. Doesn't everybody? Maybe that's the trouble. Everybody does, and so it is no longer special. It is just a boring way of getting from here to there. The rites of passage have become the right to sue if your baggage is lost or you are bumped because of overbooking. And when was legalese ever as spine-tingling as the sound of an ocean liner's basso profundo farewell or the laugh of the airline hostess who shared your excitement on your first flight.

Even on Sunday in Switzerland

There is something about the Swiss. Everything they make runs smoothly: the silken river of chocolate in a spotless factory camouflaged to look like a chateau, the famous watches and cuckoo clocks and, as we discovered, the rural police.

I had not been back to French-speaking Switzerland since I had spent a year in Geneva as a small child. My husband and I were in Zurich briefly a few years ago, but we decided this time that we would fly directly to Geneva, rent a car, drive along the north shore of Lake Geneva to Montreux, go up over the mountains to Grindelwald, and then west to Neuchatel and back to Geneva.

Luck was with us as we flew into Geneva. Mont Blanc, notoriously shy about public appearances, flaunted its pure white peak against a cloudless blue sky. The Grand Saleve, Rousseau's statue, and the muets were all just where I had left them fifty years ago. The pink horse chestnuts were in bloom and swans were nesting along the quai—my childhood memories hadn't been fantasies after all.

So we rented a car and headed up the lake. We saw vertical vineyards on our left and discretely hidden villas on our right, hugging the shores of that deep, incredibly blue lake. Through the ancient towns of Nyon, Rolle and Lausanne we drove, and after a brief obeisance to Bryon's chateau at Chillon, we headed up into the alps at Aigle.

High up on the spring-green hillsides cows with bells on their necks were sprinkled like wooden toys. An occasional chalet near the road or a small hut far up on the summer pastures were right out of *Heidi*. In fact, a modern day Heidi, a bit older than Johanna Spyri's goat girl, stood by the road with a knapsack, hoping for a ride. So we stopped, and she rode with us as far as her home in Chateau d'Oex. She had been up to visit her father, who spends each summer on the mountain with their cows, taking him laundry and a few provisions and returning with a large bag of lettuces, onions, and radishes he raised in his garden patch. She encouraged my halting French with smiles and gestures, supplying the words that stuck atrophied from disuse in my throat. We began to go through travel poster villages—the dark-brown chalets decorated with carved overhanging eaves and illuminated with painted designs and window boxes spilling over with flowers. In the village squares every house had different colored shutters and window boxes.

Lake Thun was even deeper blue and more sparkling than Lake Geneva. We skirted around the edge of Interlaken and headed up the valley towards Grindelwald, the great mountains moving nearer all the time. Grindelwald is no longer the simple unspoiled village of my childhood, but mercifully the tour buses leave by mid-afternoon, and no amount of tourism can erode the majesty of the Eiger and the Wetterhorn towering over the village.

The next day we followed the north shore of Lake Thun, by-passed Bern which we had visited before, and stopped for hot chocolate in a patisserie in Aarberg, one of the most picturesque and unpublicized towns in that part of Switzerland. Each stone house around the cobblestone square had different shaped and colored shutters, and all the window boxes were gay with geraniums.

Our destination was the Novotel in Neuchatel Est. We assumed that meant it was east of Neuchatel. But on the outskirts of the city there was a detour for road construction, so we bumped along soon finding ourselves in the heart of downtown Neuchatel. We continued through the city, looking in vain for a sign to the motel. Soon we were on the west side of town, stopped again by more road construction. We knew we had gone too far, but the traffic was only one way on a divided highway. It was impossible to get on the road going the other way. After driving nearly ten miles southwest, there was an exit and an access road to get on the east-bound lane. We retraced our path through the city.

It was Sunday. All shops and most gas stations were closed. It was raining so hard that no one was on the streets. Finally, we came to a gas station where the proprieter, obviously in his Sunday clothes and not open for business, was going over his books. He knew no English. My French petered out after, "Pardon, monsieur, est-ce que vous pouvez montrer moi sur la carte ou est le Novotel?"

He leaped up gazed heavenward, and after divine consultation announced, "Non, non, non. Ce n'est pas en Neuchatel. Mais attendez un moment." He rushed out into the rain and stopped a man on the street, and with flamboyant gestures, increasing agitation, and mounting decibles on both sides, they argued the possibility of the existance of such a motel, decided (according to the gestures) that it was probably east of Neuchatel, which we had already assumed.

59

So we continued east, bumping over the construction once more, but there was no sign of a motel or any other place where we could ask for directions. By this time we had used up over an hour, a lot of nervous energy, and at least 3 liters of gasoline. The rain and fog reduced the visibility so even if there had been a sign we probably would have missed it. Finally, on a side road off the highway, I spotted a police station. It didn't look too active, but there was one police car in the parking lot, so I fervently hoped its driver was inside.

The sign on the glass door said, "Tirez," but the door was locked. There was a bell with a sign "Poussez," so I poussed. No response, so I poussed again. Far back down a long corridor I saw a door open, and a rotund elderly gendarme trotted out, hastily squeezing himself into his blue jacket. After struggling with the bolts and locks for several minutes, while shouting through the door that on Sunday it was their custom to lock the doors, he opened the door with a flourish, bowed low and murmered, "A votre service, madame."

"Nous cherchons le Novotel, Neuchatel est," I stammered.

"Ah, Novotel, ah oui, oui," and his arms flailed the air with direction signals. "A droit, prenez garde, a gauche, kilometres." Routes and place names flew around my head like dancing lights.

"Si vous montrez—moi sur la carte?" I pleaded wistfully.

Whereupon he looked abashed, hit himself vigorously on the forehead with the back of his hand and shouted, "Jean Pierre" at the top of his lungs.

Jean Pierre—young and handsome with the high-Swiss coloring and a uniform that must have been reserved for special Sundays to impress middle-aged American ladies—appeared on the run, doffed his cap, clicked his heels, bowed low, and shook my hand.

60

"Je ne parle pas bien Francais." I croaked. "Ou est le Novotel?"

"Mais non, madame. Vous parlez tres bien Francais. Vous etes tres gentile!" And with that he opened the door with a flourish, steered me by the elbow to our car, bowed to George and pointed to the police car. "Suivez-moi, madame et monsieur, suivez-moi."

A police escort! Our spirits soared. George was hard put to follow his flashing lights as he whirled out of the parking lot, sped across the highway, over a bridge, squealed around corners on two wheels, until suddenly, looming in front of us, was a large sign which read "Novotel."

We hadn't expected it to be this near. Should we offer him a tip? How much? Before we had a chance to reconnoitre and sort out the franc notes, we were at the entrance to the motel. Jean Pierre lifted his cap in a sweeping gesture, flashed his white teeth, and was gone in a puff of carbon monoxide. I rolled down the window and shouted, "Merci, monsieur," but the rain blew the words in my face.

No wonder the Red Cross chose the Swiss flag, with reversed colors, for their emblem. The Swiss have been rescuing weary travellers with St. Bernard dogs since the Middle Ages. I forgot to look for the keg of brandy around Jean Pierre's neck.

The Odd Couple

You've heard of the Kentucky race horse that had to have his mascot, a small goat, in the stall with him for emotional stability. And there was a moose in Nova Scotia who developed a romantic attachment to a fog horn. I can remember my mother telling about a bantam hen who slept on their carriage horse's back.

But in Underhill, Vermont, one summer there was an even odder couple. When the Hensels built their new house on a mountain top, they constructed a pond which was not only swimmable but an aesthetic addition to the spectacular view from their deck. A neighbor, Joan Cross, gave the pond a christening present of a large, vinyl, inflated dolphin. He had a Mona Lisa smile and Carol Channing eyelashes and bobbed around on the pond, almost standing on his tail as though he were just about to leap out of the water. Charming as "Dolphy" was, there was nothing unique about him that couldn't be bought from Hammacher Schlemmer by any pool owner who succumbed to his seductive expression.

Towards the end of the summer, Dolphy was joined by a Canada goose who swam to his side, talked to him in confidential tones, and followed him wherever the wind carried his inflated form. When the prevailing breeze held the dolphin for

a while against some rocks at the inlet of the pond, th
fed on the grassy bank nearby. He looked to be taking c.
some necessary preening and grooming, but in fact he
keeping a watchful eye on his plastic pond-pal in case he to.
off behind his back. When a sudden squall sent Dolphy
scudding across the pond, the goose squawked, flapped his
wings, and set off after him, scolding him soundly for his
independence. For three or four weeks the two were never
apart, not by symbiosis, but by the unilateral, constant
monitoring by the goose. Frank Hensel would sometimes pick
up Dolphy and pretend to carry him away. Immediately the
goose would squonk and chase after him with outspread
wings and neck extended, hissing loudly in protest.

He slept as close as possible to his friend, whose plastic
eyelids never drooped, and all his waking hours were spent
in wing reach of the dolphin.

As the leaves began to turn, *Branta Canadensis* turned a
deaf ear to the call of high-flying wedges of wild geese arrowing
south overhead, plainly audible to the feathered-half of this
pair. His heart belonged to Dolphy, and he never so much as
ka-ronked in response to the blandishments of his own kind.

Fran Howe, the TV Bird Lady of Burlington, Vermont, and
her photographer husband Larry came to see and photograph
the odd couple. Ronald Rood, the naturalist, and Betsy
Schenk, the nature artist, also paid their respects. Jim Stewart,
the state ornithologist, was consulted, and he reported that
there was no precedent for such behavior.

But the course of true love rarely runs smoothly, and the
rocks at the edge of the pond gradually eroded a spot on
Dolphy's sleek side. One morning Dolphy's skin lay floating
on the surface, deflated and limp. Frank Hensel took it up to
the house in spite of the goose's protests and tried to mend

63

es. It seemed to work temporarily, but soon after that y was down for the count. The goose mourned his dead d, honking and trying to talk it back to life. After a few ys of grieving, he seemed to accept the fact that his rotound nd flirting friend was nothing more than a limp plastic shell. Dolphy, as he had known him, was no more, and the goose had no further reason to stay. One morning he was gone. Had he gone to the wildlife refuge in Vergennes where other Canada geese winter over, or was he on the long, lonely flight south to join his own kind?

Nothing so ambitious. He went south all right, but only three miles as the goose flies. He was found paddling around on the Danforth's pond. There are other ponds in the area, both natural and man-made, but the special attraction of this pond was a wooden duck decoy that Joan and Eliot Danforth had set out to attract wild ducks. They hadn't figured on a goose but welcomed him and fed him for several days. One evening they returned from town and found only their wooden decoy. What they also found were large boot prints all around the edge of their pond, mute evidence of the probable end of this goose tale.

But hope for this unique bird's life rose when a neighbor claimed the footsteps as his own, left when he had come to admire the odd couple.

The goose never returned. Perhaps his internal radar told him that if his man-made friends were too earthbound to go south for the winter, he might as well go on by himself. After all, the attractiveness of his first love was simply the product of inflation, and the second proved to have a wooden heart. Perhaps he has found a friendly flamingo in some park in Florida or better yet a real live goose who knows that love is not just a Mother Goose tale.

Further Goose Tales

In my previous book *Seasoned in Vermont*, I wrote a chapter about geese, but in the year's lapse between pencilled pages and actual publication of the book, our goose census and goose sense have undergone dramatic changes.

Let's see, at the last colloqium of goose talk we had four African geese: a large domineering male, two females and "Bruce Goose," the gosling that was hatched in our meadow. Bruce, as the youngest and tenderest ended up on the Christmas table just like the one Bob Crachit carved in Dickens' *Christmas Carol*. Neither of us had the desire or the courage to do him in, so we drove forty miles to Grand Isle to enlist the services of Tim Lynch. When Bruce reappeared wrapped for the freezer, he no longer looked like a part of our family. He wasn't especially tender, but I have experimented since and found that a day or two of aging and then marinating before braising results in a more toothsome product. It's all dark meat, of course, but I prefer dark meat. This, no doubt, came about because as the youngest child when we had company the white meat got pretty scarce before my plate reached the head of the table. My mother insisted that her favorite parts of the fowl were the back and neck. I thought she unselfishly asked for the least meaty parts, but now I know that, though meagre, the tastiest bits are the "oysters" on the back and the scraps on the neck, if you are willing to gnaw and suck on it like Henry VIII.

Back to geese. After Bruce's demise, we were left with three. One winter night we heard a commotion in the goose pasture, but by the time George disentangled himself from the clutches of Morpheus, pulled on his pants and boots, and got a flashlight, all he could see were tracks and a wide-swept path through the snow disappearing beyond the fence into the woods. The light of the next day revealed one female gone— no feathers, no blood. The fox or raccoon (probably a fox, in the coldest part of the winter, our resident raccoons are usually sleeping off their summer fat in a hollow tree) had dragged the goose well into the woods, and the snow was too deep to follow the tracks.

The male goose and the remaining female ignored the whole incident and displayed neither grief nor anxiety. But a few nights later, there was another uproar in the meadow, and this time George saw some thing or things going over the fence. The crusted snow was so deep that the fence wasn't much of a deterrent, and a goose wouldn't offer much resistance if the fox had him by the neck. We have learned that foxy maneuver ourselves through trial and error in goose-herding. A goose held by a hind leg is a living windmill, but if you curl your fingers around his neck, loosely but firmly, he has all the passivity of a folded umbrella.

The gander didn't take the goose-napping of his remaining companion lightly. He honked and squawked the rest of the night and the next day, until he made himself hoarse. Then he set out on a tame goose chase over the fence and down to

66

the brook, disappearing for the rest of the greater part of that day. He would return somewhat worn and very hungry only to disappear again. When he was gone for five days, we thought we had seen the last of him, until a neighbor phoned to say that there was a goose just sitting in the woods east of our house. We went up the road and found a place where there were goose tracks and foot prints, but no goose. Maybe someone had considered it a sitting duck and, thinking it wild or tasty or both, had taken him home.

Then one day Susan Latchem, down the road, called to ask if one of our geese was missing. Their neighbor's dog had caught a goose and bitten it, but it had been rescued alive and was now nursing its wounds in their woodshed. So we went over in the truck, and George sat out in the back of the truck holding the bleeding goose while I drove home. His wound was not serious, and in a day or two he was strutting around honking for his lost love.

He came and went at will, his not ours, sometimes over the fence when the snow was deep, sometimes pushing through a widened spot as the snow melted. A visiting nurse stopped to tell us our goose was down the road. Another time a whole family, parents and children, had shooed him as far as our driveway. He spent a week as a barn guest at the Neill's before they heard we had a peripatetic goose and called us up. Almost daily someone would stop to say, "Your goose is loose." When this happened a few minutes after we had brought him home or just when dinner was ready, we thanked the informant but guiltily sat down to dinner and let the gander worry about himself.

The obvious solution was to get him another female companion from the Wheelers. I know that Canada geese mate for life but we didn't know if African geese are equally monogamous. He accepted the new goose, and they seemed content to stay around the home place for a day or two. But he had had a taste of freedom and apparently wanted to show his new friend that there was life beyond their fenced-in pasture. They both disappeared, and I secretly hoped that that was the end of that goose chapter. No such luck. Isabella Martin, who lives a few miles from us, phoned to say that there were two geese in their meadow and might they be ours? They were, of course, and we were able to catch the tired female and put her in a crate in the back of the truck. The male led us on a merry chase up to our ankles in a muddy swamp, and the best we could do was get him out on the road. So George shooed him down Field's Lane with me driving the truck in low gear behind them. After a mile or two we swapped roles, and I shooed while George drove at goose-step pace. Cars passed our little procession, their occupants staring and smirking but kindly refraining from tapping their heads. But when we reached Fred Casey's open field, the goose took off into the middle of the field. We left him to his own devices and went on home with the female, hoping he'd find his way home to his new friend. He did come home but only stayed a few a days, and then wanderlust came over them again.

By now it was spring. In one of the homing intervals, the goose had laid several eggs which we took to the Wheeler's incubator. I had mixed feelings and half hoped they wouldn't hatch, but four out of the five did. Now we had a new problem. With the parents once again in absentia, who would take care of the goslings? Obviously they would require adult geese as guardians, so once again we enlisted Thelma and Jack Wheeler's help, and they gave us a gander and a lame goose named Jill, who was reputed to make up in maternal instincts what she lacked in agility. Jack, Thelma, George, and I stood by the fence when we put the new arrivals in the pasture. Instantly the male rushed around the periphery, poking and pushing at the fence, and on the far side before any of us could reach him, he shoved himself through a widened spot in the fence and took off to parts unknown. Within twenty-four hours, Jill came tumbling after and neither was seen again.

The Wheelers generously kept the goslings until they outgrew their heated brooder, and then George built them a fenced-in cage inside the barn that was about as hard to break into as Fort Knox. You think I'm going to say they got out of that, don't you? Nope. They grew to maturity, graduated to an outdoor pen made with smaller mesh wire, and are now tucked away in the freezer. Do we plan to have more geese next spring? Are you crazy? We may be slow learners, but we've seen the goose tracks on the wall, and they indicate that geese and Wolfs are incompatible.

Let's Stop for
a Sandwich

In spite of the popularity of fish and chips, crepes, quiches, and sushi bars, the most ubiquitous item of food in the American diet remains the sandwich. We consider the Big Mac, stadium hot dogs, and peanut butter and jelly sandwiches as indigenous as apple pie and football.

But oddly enough the sandwich is not a North American invention. It was dreamed up by John Montague, known as "Jemmy Twitcher," the 4th Earl of Sandwich, who lived from 1718 to 1792. As Lord of the Admiralty, his "corruption and incapacity was unique in the history of the British Navy." His bad management contributed to the failure of the British fleet in our Revolution. But he did bequeath us the sandwich. Because he was wont to spend twenty-four hours a day at the gaming tables and was unwilling to stop for a proper dinner, he ordered cold beef between slices of toast, which he could hold in one hand while clutching his cards or dice in the other.

Over the next 200 years the sandwich in England became refined almost to extinction in the form of miniscule, cucumber tea sandwiches that daintily sustained the British ladies through that long interval between lunch and dinner.

But the concept of the sandwich is international. Morsels of lamb are tucked into the pouches of pita bread in the Near East. Reuben sandwiches of corned beef, sauerkraut, and Swiss cheese became popular in New York delicatessens. Smorbrod (bread and butter) or smorgasbord gained favor in the Scandinavian countries. Window displays of open-faced sandwiches of tiny shrimp and dill, herring, or cold meat along the walking street in Copenhagen are irresistable. Mexico has tacos and tortillas. Egg rolls are a form of sandwich. Crusty loaves of Italian bread were filled with sausage, olive oil, tomatoes, and anchovies, a forerunner of the Hero sandwich, which has been known to be six feet long and capable of serving thirty people. Thin slices of Smithfield ham on beaten biscuits in the South, piles of barbecued meat on buns in the Midwest, cream cheese and lox on bagels for Sunday breakfast in New York, show regional preferences.

But from sea to shining sea, every red-blooded American child cuts his molars on "peem burr and jeddy samwiches." When our children catapulted from the school bus, down the driveway, and into the kitchen, their goal was peanut butter which they spread liberally over the counter and their faces as well as the bread.

Mrs. Appleyard (Louise Andrews Kent) once wrote to me about her disappointment that we were not going to be in Vermont at the same time one summer. "Oh well, as my youngest grandson said instead of crying, when he dropped a confection he had just carefully made of peanut butter and marshmellow fluff face down on the floor. I have now adopted this philosophy, but though I found it helpful, it seems arid for this deprivation."

Dagwood Bumstead is the dean of American sandwich makers. His leaning towers of everything defy the ability of the human jaw to encompass them without dislocation. When George was having teeth problems, he envied anyone who could bite and chew with comfort. We are not a nation of sippers and nibblers. Apparently we need to work out some of our aggressions with our bare teeth.

And most of all we like to hold food in our hands. I must admit to having trouble keeping the contents of a taco inside its crisp container rather than exploding them all over my lap, and my smallest grandson likes to separate a sandwich and take out the filling for closer inspection before cramming it into his mouth with both hands. Is there an adult holding this book who did not pry open oreo sandwiches as a child and lick off the white filling?

Some of the worst sandwiches in the world are the pre-wrapped and chilled offerings in self-service glass cases in airports. The bread must be kneaded with large amounts of absorbent cotton. The pallid chicken or ham is thin to the point of transparency, and there is no visible trace of butter or any other emollient. I suppose they operate on the premise that you are about to board a plane for some remote country and will never return to retaliate.

When I recently ordered a small Hero on a bun and naively agreed to "everything" on it, I was overwhelmed when, not only the meat, but onion rings, cheese, tomato, lettuce, relish, mustard, and mayonnaise all kept bulging out like vertebral discs at each bite. It tasted pretty good, but it was mechanically unmanageable. So is a club sandwich. But one of the best gastronomic memories of my childhood is my first three-decker club sandwich in the dining car of the Southern Pacific Railroad going to California. I was only six years old, but I remember the enamelled, linen napkin which skidded off my lap, the heavy "silver" ware, the ice tinkling in the glasses with each clickety-clack of the wheels, and the beautiful treat before me. There were layers and layers of white-meat chicken, crisp bacon, red ripe tomatoes, and lettuce curling seductively from the edges, all anchored together with toothpicks that had little frilly pantaloons on them. And wonder of wonders, three ripe olives on the side! Now there was a sandwich that probably exists only in the remembrance of things past, like Proust's Madeleines. The fact that it was grown-up fare and in a grown-up portion enhanced its glamour. And the additional benefit was that it was perfectly legal and expected that I should pick it up and eat it with my fingers.

We haven't evolved as far as we pretend from the medieval manner of eating with only the occasional services of a knife to whack off a hunk of meat. Our tribal memories still stir in our subconscious. If we can't go on a picnic or camp out daily, at least we can pretend to by eating a sandwich.

Lord of the Flies

Among the lifelong ambitions to which we do not aspire is the care and feeding of the cluster fly. Job had his locusts and so did Salt Lake City. In fact, when the sea gulls moved in and ate all the locusts, the Mormons were so grateful that they erected a monument to them. Now I'm not much for monuments, with the exception of Copenhagen's little mermaid and perhaps the Lincoln and Jefferson Memorials, but I would at least crash a few cymbals for someone who could exterminate the house fly.

When cows were pastured on our land, we had a lot of big flies which we tried to keep on the far side of our doors and windows. The old Vermont custom of sticking bits of absorbent cotten on screen doors always looked pretty silly to me, like a man's face on a morning when his dexterity with the razor was not up to par. I just can't see why a fly would be repelled by tufts of cotton. But they say an elephant is afraid of a mouse, so who am I to argue with tradition?

After cows were no longer on our land, and we had planted our fields to white pine, the barn flies took to more fragrant pastures, and except for the occasional vicious attack of a bomber-shaped deer fly, or the sneaky black flies in the spring, we could work out our aggressions on barn rats, garden woodchucks, and corn-loving raccoons.

That is, we could in the average year. But in Vermont years don't seem to run true to expectations. I mean you go along with your usual last frost on May 20, or thereabouts, and the first frost around September 20 for several years, and then the next year your tomato plants are killed on June 10th, or your pole beans turn translucent on the last day of August. Normally we have snow on the ground from mid-November till April Fools' Day, but in the winter of 1982-83 there was almost no snow in December. It was 50° in January, and the ski people were ready to leap off the mountains like lemmings.

So I should not be surprised that the cluster fly population varies from year to year. They are probably always with us, or at least they produce the same number of larvae. It takes a sudden warmth after cold to bring them out in clouds.

One year when our house in Jericho was used only in the summer, we came from Kansas for a fall week-end. Debbie and a friend, Bruce Thorsen, came up from New York to share the beauty of the foliage season. We started up the stove in the old house to warm it up and dry it out. But it wasn't only the dampness that came out. Cluster flies by the hundreds crept out of the chinks in the old walls and ceiling, bumping into us in mid-air, whirling in their intermittent dance of death on the window sills and tables, and crunching underfoot. We swatted and finally sprayed the whole interior of the house, and they dropped like guess what. We swept them up in heaps, but it also did Debbie's boyfriend in. We had no idea that he was allergic to the insecticide. His eyes and nose ran. His face was swollen and he could hardly breath. No surprise that the romance did not endure, though I'm glad to report that Bruce is alive and well on Wall Street, where the bulls and bears don't attract flies.

When we built the new house, we thought that because it

was tight and new and well insulated the cluster flies would not be part of our winter census. As a matter of fact, for several winters there were only a few of them whirling like dervishes.

But in the winter of 1982-83, we had several very warm spells after the first cold weather. The lilac buds tried to come out. So did the flies. We vacuumed them up around the windows with the hand vacuum three times a day. Several hundred had to be hand-picked out of the thick carpet, and "still we gazed and still the wonder grew."

When they began dropping into the food as I was cooking, sterner measures had to be taken. We are not keen on insecticides, but it began to look as though it was the flies or us. A neighbor told us that her vet had suggested a bomb that successfully rid their house of fleas. We figured that what's good for a flea ought to be good for a fly. You had to shut up the house, set off the bomb, vacate the house for two hours, and then air it for half an hour before settling in once more.

I was doing a stint as a volunteer at the Old Mill Craft Shop, so George got the duty. When I came home he was vacuuming up large areas where the gold carpet was black with flies.

You may expect that I am going to say that that was the end of the flies. That's what we expected and fervently hoped. It did slow them down a bit, and a cold spell sent them into hiding as is their wont, but the next sunny day guess who came to dinner and lunch and breakfast?

Where do they hide? We have never seen them emerging from the windows. We have no attic to harbor them. Now that it is really cold, we are enjoying a respite, but with no assurance that along with the ides of March and the warmth of the spring sun George won't regain his latest title as Lord of the Flies.

This Is Not a Recording

I can't believe I am the only one who is intimidated by recorded answering services. When the voice, real enough but somehow disembodied like the ghost in *Blithe Spirit*, intones, "I am not at home right now. At the sound of the beep please leave your message and your name and phone number." I am suddenly stricken dumb.

Under normal circumstances I am a verbal artesian well. I sometimes believe that I write because I realize I can't expect to rivet the attention of my friends and relations indefinitely. I can see their eyes begin to glaze over as they yearn to get out of my life and on with their own. My small grandson Morgan, with uncanny prescience, named me "Blabby" instead of "Grandma" long before he knew the meaning of the word. In fact he still does, and he still doesn't. That's spooky, but it convinces me that that child will go far—and of course Morgan is one of the three most remarkable little boys in the world.

But just let me hear a recording instead of a live voice that has two ears and a body and I am overcome with the urge to replace the phone as silently as possible lest by the least breath I reveal my identity.

The sensation reminds me of an incident when I was in the fifth grade. We had a class in Arts and Crafts. It was presided over by a solemn, mannish sort of woman who obviously would have preferred to be almost anywhere else. I had not heard of paranoia at that tender age, but she had it. One day a classmate whispered something to me, and I whispered back. Miss Vincent fixed me with a baleful eye and demanded that I tell the class what my friend and I had said. I was stricken dumb. My mouth opened and shut convulsively but not a word came out. Finally the wrath of both Miss Vincent and God loosened my paralysed tongue. "Betty said that everybody hates you but I said I didn't think you were THAT bad."

Did I get rewarded for my honesty or even for sticking up for her? I did not. She called upon my mother and insisted that I apologize to her and again in front of the class. I hadn't heard of masochism either, but I could tell she wasn't doing a thing for her image.

Now the recorded message isn't accusing me of anything, is it? Why does it make me feel like I am trespassing, breaking and entering the house of the person I am calling, and that I'd prefer to get out as quickly and quietly as possible?

I can give an extemporaneous speech to a live audience with only minimal increase in my pulse rate. I can face a classroom of fifth graders without a qualm. But I can manage a TV interview only by looking at the interviewer and NEVER looking at the monitor. I learned the hard way. The first time I did occasionally sneak a quick glance at the monitor, and I discovered a strangely familiar but unattractive woman making grimaces and gesticulating like a Sicilian street vendor. But at least with the TV interview you do have a human being to speak to. He is alive and making a noble effort to seem interested. The phone recording has no persona.

If I must live in the age of depersonalization, I suppose I can learn at least to identify myself—name, rank, and serial number; but I doubt if I'll ever be able to live up to my name as "Blabby."

Fall

Fall in Vermont is a clarion call to all five senses. If a Vermonter is temporarily exiled to another state, the mention of fall will evoke memories of the taste, smell, sound, light, and color. But being in the middle of it is an intense sensory experience. We never believe that it can be so dramatic and yet find that each annual performance merits new superlatives.

People from "away" often say, "I suppose you get used to all this color and don't notice it." Nope. The Vermonter revels and wallows in it, storing up light and color to sustain him through sub-zero winter nights and the sloughs of mud season. He takes a day off from filling the silo or digging late potatoes to check out remembered spots of glory. There is fierce debate at the post office as to the location of the best color, yet no one can claim victory, because it is impossible to drive through every golden tree tunnel or to count the phalanxes of flaming maples marching up the hillsides. You must seize the moment, because tomorrow may bring a pelting rain that will loosen the glistening leaves and spread them like oriental rugs under the trees.

You can feel fall coming. On an August night when you dislocate your neck watching for a falling star, you will feel a chill in the air. The swimming pool in the brook is noticeably colder, and when you bring a pumpkin in from the garden, its hard, orange rind is as cool as marble to the touch.

There is a new scent of asters and goldenrod, more mellow than the barely discernable fragrance of mid-summer chicory and Queen Anne's lace. As September slips into October there are richer smells: the inside of a pumpkin, a basket of apples, chili sauce simmering on the stove, the acrid scent of burning leaves, and the maple-flavored essence of wood smoke. When fall drowses towards winter, the smells of rotting leaves and bruised windfalls are sweet, musty, earthy, truffly scents. I've never smelled a truffle, but certainly this is the scent that guides the pigs in the oak forests of France to that culinary treasure.

Harvest smells are also the taste of fall: green tomato mincemeat, bread and butter pickles redolent of vinegar and spices, cucumbers, onions, and green peppers. The whole church basement on the night of the annual chicken pie supper is fragrant with coffee, which lures you to the soul-satisfying flavors of biscuit-topped chicken pie rich with golden gravy, crisp cole slaw, mountains of mellow winter squash, and mashed potatoes. This is all topped off by tart-sweet apple pies or the ubiquitous pumpkin.

Fall has distinctive sounds, starting with the resumed rumble of the big, yellow school buses filled with squealing children and the sound of the corn chopper harvesting long rows of field corn for the silos. One morning when you walk to the garden, the frosted grass crunches and skids beneath your feet, and the corn leaves have a more brittle sound in the breeze. But the sound that lifts your heart and your eyes skyward is the distant baying of Canada geese arrowing south, almost

invisible at first and only briefly audible. It's a wild, strange chorus that is as evocative of fall as the first peepers are of spring.

But of course what one remembers most on the inward eye is the ever-changing, ever-contrasting color. There is an opaline quality on early September mornings when the mists are still tucked in around the river valleys. As the day progresses every back road lined with luminous golden sugar maples seems to surround you with light and even reflect it in the golden pools underfoot. The red swamp maples are the first to ignite, and the intensity of their scarlet and vermilion is in sharp contrast to the other still-green deciduous trees. But as they fade, the sugar maples, the lemon yellow popple and birch, the darker gold beech, and the wine-red oaks join in the conflagration until the whole hillsides are vibrant with a kaleidoscope of color.

It can't be true! But it is, here and now. It can never happen again. But it will. Each year we wait and hope. Each year it is a promise fulfilled.

"And Sealing Wax"

Whatever happened to sealing wax? I came across a little box of it in a bureau drawer, and it brought back memories of grade school and rainy afternoons. My friends Janet, Helena, and I would spend hours melting our little bars of sealing wax and trying to get a perfect imprint by pressing the blobs of melted wax with our seals.

We never actually sealed anything except an occasional thank-you letter to our grandmothers after Christmas, but we had a lot of fun, and I can still smell the hot wax and see the lovely colors of the bars—silver and emerald green, gold and bright red.

Sealing wax was used to seal letters before there were envelopes with gummed flaps. In fact, an envelope closed with sealing wax was tamperproof, because a broken seal could not be camouflaged. We found very old letters in our attic in South Burlington that had been sealed with red sealing wax. They were dated from 1787 to1810. I'm not sure when the envelope came into general use. A letter was just folded and a blob of hot wax dropped on the cut edge. Then the warm wax was stamped with the seal. Royalty and prominent persons had seal rings to stamp their correspondence in the days when letter writing was an art as well as the chief form of communication. Seals, usually without wax, are still used to emboss important documents. Every notary uses a seal. Colleges and universities have seals, and so does each state and country, though they are primarily used for ceremonial purposes. The expression "signed and sealed" turns up on many legal documents and is one of the few expressions in legalese that I can understand.

The stamps that we used as children had inverted initials on the metal end and then a wooden handle like any other stamp. In the little box I found there were several stamps with both an M and an H. I remember those as my own. And along with the tiny candle stick, several birthday-cake-size candles, and two partly used bars of wax there was a small, sterling silver seal with an Old English H on it. Now that has more status than my little stamps. Did it belong to my paternal grandmother? It was tarnished, but I polished it up, and it shines like a little piece of jewelry. That's one piece of silver that was not stolen when everything else made of silver went out out window in one of our pillow cases.

What was the fascination of sealing wax for us as children? It was more than just the fun of playing with a tiny amount of fire. It was partly that a seal makes something private and personal. When you put your initial on something, you lay claim to it. Why do you suppose monogrammed everything—luggage, shirts, silver—is so popular? We are territorial like animals and birds. We like to say "Mine!" loudly, like Morgan my three-year-old grandson does. He now wants to be more than a passive baby. He is a person to be reckoned with, with his possessions clearly "signed and sealed." You pay five dollars more to have your monogram embroidered on a sweater. But we know from sad experience that a monogram on flat silver does not prevent it from being stolen, because it is melted down within twenty-four hours.

I wonder if monograms are popular in China or Russia. In America, and especially in Vermont, independence and ownership are still respected, and I have no intention of throwing away that little sealing wax set.

More About Men
and Women

In an earlier book I wrote a chapter called, "Why Can't a Man Be More Like a Woman?" It dealt with several nearly universal differences. Men don't like to ask directions. Women do. Men don't like to shop for clothes. Women do. A woman may pack the suitcases indoors, but the man packs them into the car and hides, way back in the farthest recesses, whatever will be needed first (the lunch basket and the overnight bags) "because they fit in better that way." And then there is the eternal male wail, "Where did YOU put my Legos set? or hockey stick, or fishing flies?" Does a female ever ask, "Where did you put my Gucci bag?" Never.

But when I give a talk somewhere and mention these emotionally-charged, if not earth-shaking differences, I will see someone in the audience jerk back from dreamland and nod in vigorous agreement. After the talk, up she'll trot as fast as she can caper with a variation on the same theme, and invariably it will be something that happens in our house, too.

For instance, breathes there a man with soul so dead who never to his wife has said, "I can't find anything in your pocketbook?" Now I'll admit that when our children were small, my pocketbook might contain, in addition to the male-approved complement of money, keys, credit cards, and license, a few accretions like one soggy mitten, two half-sucked lollipops permanently attached to a tissue, three PTA bulletins, four jacks minus ball, five raffle tickets to raise money for the band uniforms, no partridges, and not one pear tree. Where was I supposed to put that flotsam and jetsam? When I was small I used to stash all my acquisitions in my voluminous bloomers, because they were anchored firmly to my legs by inserted elastic tape. Of course if I passed a horse chestnut tree with just-opened, glistening, waxy chestnuts and squirreled them away, my bloomers began to drag a bit, and pedalling home on my bike was a knobby and rattly business. But bloomers are no longer part of my wardrobe, and I no longer feel compelled to take every horse chestnut home. Maybe a few shells from Longboat Key and perhaps a key lime or two.

A man is supplied with pockets everywhere, four or five on his jacket and at least two in his pants—and that's before he has put on his top coat. Yet every man I know, if asked to get something out of his wife's handbag, pales visibly, holds the offending reticule at arm's length, marches to the nearest table, and dumps the entire contents out, exposing her life's secrets like the layers in an archaeological dig.

It is not only her pocketbook that reduces him to temporary blindness. How about the refrigerator? With the door wide open air-conditioning the kitchen on a hot day, he stands in front of it, peering suspiciously into various containers with an expression on his face that suggests the next one may contain a dead mouse or some razor blades she has been saving for his birthday cake. The idea of using up the opened milk carton or the bologna package before starting on a new one remains a mystery to him.

Ice cube trays are my husband's special nemesis. Although he handles them daily, he is incapable of emptying an ice cube tray into the ice cube storage container without sending a third of them skidding across the floor. Now this is the same man who hangs up his clothes, sweeps the garage floor, and is positively compulsive about the arangement of his bureau drawers. The obvious solution is an automatic ice cube maker and dispenser, but we are already so mechanized with a combination coffee bean grinder and coffee maker, toaster oven, blender, can opener, mixer, self-cleaning oven, self-defrosting refrigerator, that I really think a man with enough dexterity to replace a tiny part on the coffee bean grinder ought to be able to aim the ice cubes more accurately.

And speaking of dexterity, why is it that women are born with the ability to thread a needle and remove a splinter, while both these skills elude most men during their entire lifetime?

Men are also congenitally unable to hear a baby's cry in the night or the sound of rain pelting against screened-but-open windows. Of course this is protective deafness, and I suppose the survival of the species depends on someone sleeping through the night. Although George complains of insomnia, I have to shake, rattle, and roll him out of bed, if someone who has skidded into the ditch in front of our house is pounding on our door in the middle of the night.

Sam Rowley, a pediatrician friend with a sensitive ear for heart murmurs and other bruits in his small patients, could sit in his living room reading calmly while his five children and our two were tearing each other limb from limb. When Jane Rowley would finally shout from upstairs, "Sayam!" he would surface slowly up out of his deep dream of peace and survey the carnage with genuine surprise.

Under the heading "Men are unlikely to" we can add: remember the names of their neighbors' children, the addresses of their own grown children, the dates of their own grandchildren's birthdays, or vital bits of local information, such as pregnancy, boyfriends, or marriage (hopefully not in that order).

A woman rarely says to her spouse, "You wouldn't understand." but it comes to his lips as naturally as "What's for dinner?" It is also guaranteed to make her want to deposit whatever IS for dinner on the top of his head.

Men are not inferior. They are just different. And lest you think I am guilty of misandry (the opposite of misogeny), I have to admit there are many areas in which men excel. Let me name a few. For instance, I am delighted that George follows the stock market closely, at least the portion of it that sends us dividends. He can also decipher an income tax form that overwhelms me with a feeling of inadequacy. In general, men are more knowledgeable about the internal workings of cars, radios, and chain saws, for which I am grateful. They saw and lug better, hammer nails straighter, and are less alarmed by things that go bump in the night.

Wait a minute. I've left out something that they are not good at, and that is waiting—be it for five minutes or an hour. All children hate to wait for shoelaces to be tied, for food to be prepared, or for grownups to stop talking on the phone. But somewhere along the line, women are programmed to wait, willy nilly, and it is nilly for a long time. But after years of waiting in an obstetrician's office, for a child's music lesson to be over, at the airport for her husband's plane which is still in a holding pattern, or for him when he becomes mesmerized in a hardware store, she finally learns that in spite of the pause that depresses he is well worth waiting for.

Women's Rites

I'm all for women's rights as long as I don't have to march in front of the State House or in a picket line, but women's rites amuse and confuse me and even occasionally make me wish I'd been born a boy.

Fortunately, many of the social formalities that my mother accepted as gracious living are now obsolete. I don't mourn the passing of card trays, the "at home" afternoons, the finger bowls, white gloves and flowered hats that were de rigueur right up through the 20's. I haven't seen a corset cover, a "rat," or a hat pin since I was in the 4th grade, and my children wouldn't know what they were for if they did see them. But we are not as free from female mores as we'd like to believe.

Why do women kiss each other or at least the air adjacent to the cheek in greeting? As far as I'm concerned, kissing should be reserved for the top of the head of a toddler grandchild or the mouth of the "significant other." Women are expected to kiss their parents, but they don't like it any better than you do. Men kiss each other more than they used to, but it usually looks like a variation of back slapping after a touchdown or a home run.

What would young female entertainers do with their hands if they couldn't fiddle with their hair all the time, sweeping it back off their faces like Cher or running their fingers through it nervously in combing motions? Our grandmothers always smoothed back their hair and their skirts before meeting guests. It was a last rite before they plunged into the social arena. Men straighten their ties and pull down their shirt cuffs for the same reason. After all, a grown man can't suck his thumb, but have you noticed how often TV personalities touch the sides of their noses or chins?

Another woman's rite is dabbing perfume on her ear lobes. Is it so that the woman kissing the air near her ear will get a whiff of Chanel? Men slap their faces with after-shave lotion but never dab their ear lobes.

Why do women cover their mouths with one or both hands when they are surprised or pleased? Are they afraid that evil spirits will see them smile and take away the prize? Watch one of the winners on a TV game show. If it is a woman, you won't see the lower half of her face for the rest of program. They immediately stuff a bouquet into Miss America's hands so she won't walk down the runway with her face covered. She cries instead, but that also seems to be a woman's rite in moments of pleasure.

One of the most futile and universal of the women's rites in our culture is putting out guest towels and little sea shells of guest soap. I've been hanging up the same embroidered guest towels for forty years, and some of them have yet to feel the touch of a wet hand. I just take them out and put them back in the drawer, mindless slave that I am to tribal custom. I suspect that our guests use the underside of the bath towels, because I've never seen one waving his wet hands in the air, and I hope they don't stoop to wiping them on the bath mat.

Another rite that most women feel they have to perform is to disparage any compliment on their clothing. A woman may say a simple "thank you" if you admire her hair, decor, or children, but the minute you say, "What a lovely dress!" she feels duty-bound to exclaim, "This old thing? I've had it for years," even though the price tag is peeking out of the back of her collar. Women who have taught their children never to lie will tell a college classmate, "You haven't changed a bit!" although her friend has obviously acquired thirty pounds, two chins, and the wrinkles of sun-dried fruit. She will admire a baby that looks as though it needs another two months in utero. And she will rave about your house in the woods when you can sense she is on the watch for an Indian or a bear.

Men don't lie to flatter others. They lie to flatter themselves by creating a fantasy about their prowess in fishing finance, or romantic flings. Fortunately, few of them do it. Big boys don't need to. I don't think women have a right to distort the truth either, but right or wrong they sometimes have a rite to do it.

But what really embarrasses me is the rite of squealing or screaming. I'm not sure that I can face another college reunion, because being a non-squealer, I really felt out of it at the last one. I have never screamed in my life. I have shouted, groaned aloud, and talked non-stop, but never has a social squeal or startled scream erupted from my mouth. I think on his wedding day a man should have the right to ask his bride, "Do you solemnly swear that you will never scream or squeal as long as we both shall live under the same roof?"

Now there's a rite I would heartily endorse.

Small World

When we lived in Kansas, Patty came home one fall to recuperate from hepatitis which she had contracted in Yugoslavia. Her activity was restricted, but she spent most of her limited energy with a group called Mini-Mundo. These were wives of foreign house staff or faculty members at the Medical Center who came from India, Japan, Denmark, or Iran. What they wanted was immediate help in solving the mysteries of the laundromat or the strange sizes of clothes or unfamiliar foods in the supermarket, as well as informal companionship with their peers. One of the most nerve shattering jobs Patty took on was teaching a young Thai woman how to drive a car, when she didn't know the words for right, left, gas, or more importantly, brake.

Now, sixteen years later, Patty is a foreign wife who has lived outside the United States for the past fifteen years (thirteen in Finland and two in Denmark). She has experienced firsthand the problems of unfamiliar currency, ethnic customs, and new langauge, not as a tourist, whose gaffes are forgiven though secretly smiled at, but as a functioning, tax-paying citizen dealing with the phone company, the bank, the schools, and medical care in Finnish, Swedish, or Danish.

We visited them in their new home in Lille Vaerlose near Copenhagen and were delighted with their roomy, colorful house and big garden where cherry blossoms were sifting down on beds of tulips and daffodils. And once again, Patty has found a group of most attractive friends from Switzerland, Australia, Wyoming, and of course friendly Denmark. When I commented on how easy it was to feel at home with all of them (granted they all spoke English to us), Patty said, "There are people with the same interests and values everywhere. National origin has very little to do with it."

In our hotel on the waterfront there were tour groups from Japan, Germany, and France. On Sundays at the Tivoli most of the strollers or squealers on roller coasters were Danish, from toddlers to frail elderly people using walkers. And the sprinkling of tourists shared their pride in the spectacular flowerbeds and fountains. A little French girl was down ah-ahing over a mother duck who was trying to cover all eight of her downy ducklings at once with her wings. Flowers, baby animals, puppet shows, bands, and spun sugar speak a universal language.

"It's a small world," has a coincidental rather than a geographical meaning for us. Each time we have gone to Europe we have bumped into some friend from the United States whom we rarely see at home. In 1961 we took the girls on their first trip to Paris, and of course we went to the Eiffel Tower, Notre Dame, Mont Martre, and the Louvre. Standing in front of the Mona Lisa, mesmerized not only by that enigmatic lady but also by fatigue and museum feet, a man next to me whispered, "Hello, Wolfs." It was Mert Lamden, one of George's colleagues at the UVM Medical College.

Mary and Kenneth Schmidt have been close friends since

college days. After we moved to Vermont and they were living on Long Island, we rarely could get together. But when we went to Europe in 1971, guess who we had breakfast with at the Mayfair in London?

Jean and Fred Plum were house staff friends at New York Hospital. We had not seen them during the years they lived in Seattle and then New York City. But it seemed quite natural to see Jean waiting on the dock for us in Malmo, Sweden, when we took the flygbot over from Copenhagen.

In the spring of 1983 we had a week's visit with Patty and Tage and the boys. On the day we left I was standing guard over our luggage in the Copenhagen airport while George was exploring the duty free shops. As I stood there I heard a gentle, tentative voice ask, "Maggie? Is that you? Am I hallucinating?" It was Marie Vogelman from Jericho Center. Now Marie and I see each other about once a year even though we live in the same village, so the chances of out meeting in the Kastrup airport are about one in a million. I haven't seen her since we've been back, of course. Maybe the next time will be on the Great Wall of China.

A Wolf in Sheep's Clothing

Our youngest grandson, Morgan, who is just past three, calls our sheep "Mary-had-a-little-lambs." The fact that they are males does not concern him. It doesn't concern them either because they are only three months old and far from ramhood. Their first priority right now is trying to get into the barn where they suspect their grain is stored. At least they know that we emerge from the barn with a scoopful of grain at feeding time. What they would do if they did get into the grain room I can imagine only too well. It doesn't take much to startle the two young pigs who jump and scream even at the sight of our familiar faces, and the twenty laying hens in an area fenced off by floor to ceiling chicken wire would panic in unison, flapping and squawking in protest at the invasion of their privacy.

So the two sheep live outside of the barn but inside their fenced-in pasture. There is plenty of succulent grass for them but sheep have a built-in "the grass is always greener on the other side of the fence" complex, and they devote half of their waking hours to shoving their heads through the fence as far as they can trying to snatch mouthfuls of the out-of-bounds

98

fodder. Every sheep we have ever had has done this, even in a fresh area with short, new grass. They go on coveting greener pastures right up to their demise in November, and there is always a shorn rim a few inches wide all the way around their enclosure. I don't know if a sheep's brain is small in relation to his body size, but his intelligence is. I have known of tethered sheep who wound themselves tighter and tighter until they strangled themselves. We had a ram who felt he had to leap over a shaft of light, and the ewes following him did too.

The two we have now are very handsome, white-faced, and dainty with very soft voices. Last year we had only one Suffolk lamb and he maa-ed loudly and continously. The only voice louder on the premises was George shouting "Shut up!" at him periodically. I hope it made George feel better because it had no effect on the sheep whatsoever. We decided he was lonely, so this year we have two. They are very quiet and they maa; one is a boy soprano and the other one must have laryngitis. Perhaps this breed is low-keyed. I'll have to ask Paul and Eva Eschholz who are our sheep providers as well as the co-owners with Al and Maggie Rosa of New England Press, my publishers.

When we first became sheepish, George was dreaming of wool as well as lamb chops. He envisioned shearing the sheep himself and handing the wool over to me to card, spin and weave. That picture was definitely out of focus. Years ago he tried to shear one sheep, and the result was a sorry looking display of tufts, nicks, and bald spots. I once tried carding and decided within a few minutes that it was not my calling. I've never even tried to spin or weave, and our house is over-stuffed now without a spinning wheel or a loom.

But we did think that when the sheep was butchered we might make a sheepskin rug out of the pelt. We followed the directions, scraping and salting the underside for several days.

100

Whatever good the lanolin did for my hands was counteracted by the salt, and my hands slowly turned into something found only in an Egyptian tomb. Then George soaked the skin in a plastic can filled with a solution of oxalic acid for five days. It smelled strange and looked awful. At the end of its tanning period he draped it over a fence to drain.

The next step was to rinse it thoroughly, and the brook seemed the logical place. George soaked and swished it, but when he tried to lift it out he discovered that the thick wool had acted like a sponge. It was so water-logged that instead of pulling it out it nearly pulled him into the icy water. He dragged it onto the bank and tried to wring out some of the water. It was so heavy that the only way he could carry it up the steep hill was to drape it over his shoulder. Staggering under the weight, he was the wettest, coldest Wolf in sheep's clothing I've ever seen.

It took a week for the sheepskin to dry, and even after brushing it with a curry comb it was a grey, matted disaster. Since then we have happily rolled our salted pelts each year and mailed them off via UPS to a tannery in Pennsylvania. They return transformed from something that looks as though it should be buried into a soft, white fluffy rug at half the price of those in the mail order catalogues.

It Was Just One
of Those Days

Every once in a while a day comes along that turns out to be pure dross. They happen more frequently when you have pre-school children, days when a three-year-old squeezes out all the toothpaste just to see how much is in the tube and then tries to flush the empty tube down the toilet with the predictable result. You are heating some milk on the stove, and when you turn around to heave the cat off the counter, the milk boils all over the stove. When you try to stuff your toddler's newly-shod feet into his last year's boots you bend you fingernail backward. He then raises his head suddenly, cracking you sharply under the chin, causing you to bite your tongue. Why was your tongue hanging out? How else do you maneuver a wiggling child into winter outerwear except by working your tongue and jaw into contortions?

Well, enough of the miserable re-runs. Now that our two daughters have pre-school children of their own and they live 18 miles west of us in Debbie's case and 3,500 miles east of us in Patty's, most of our days are disaster free with only an errant turkey or firewood that won't burn to test our mettle. But even in this relatively calm phase we occasionally have a day that should have been dropped from the calendar, like when you cross the date line in the Pacific and suddenly Sunday is followed by Tuesday and Monday is lost in the briny deep.

It all started innocently enough. We drove down to Boston and had reservations at the Holiday Inn right near Massachusetts General Hospital. We knew about where it was. We lived near Boston for five years, and I used to drive George from Weston to Logan Airport at least once a week. I could see our motel from Storrow Drive. But somehow when we got off the southbound highway and tried to cut back near the North Station, we got disoriented by all the urban renewal. Streets were either one-way or no left turn, and we wandered around on the slopes of Beacon Hill like tourists unfamiliar with the maze of Boston's cowpaths. Deciding we were near enough to leave the car and find it on foot, we drove into a parking garage. The was no one at the booth and no machine spewing out tickets, so we circled up two, three, four, five ramps, hunting for a space. It was completely filled. All the way down I kept remembering that on the New York Throughway if you lose your ticket you pay the maximum toll. We had no ticket and no proof that we had been in the garage only five futile minutes. Fortunately the check-out booth was still empty, and we sailed out into the sunlight feeling somehow guilty for not having recorded our visit. Just before George's chronic resistance to asking directions broke down, we found the motel, only to be told that our room would not be ready for an hour. It was almost closing time in the coffee shop, but we squeezed in past the emerging customers, obstructing their egress with our bags, only to be glared at by the waitress who was eager to get off duty and off her feet. Much later our room was ready, and we dumped our suitcases, got washed up, and started off to see the parts of Boston that had been revamped in our absence.

But the day's curse was still upon us. No sooner had we stepped into the elevator and started down than it stopped dead between floors. You read about this happening. You joke about it. But it never happens to you. You even see it on television, with a lady going into labor in the crowded stuck elevator. We were the only occupants, and my last baby had graduated from college, but it was still a strange sensation. Neither of us is claustrophobic, but it wasn't the way we had planned to spend the afternoon. George pushed floor buttons. Nothing happened. He pushed the alarm button, and way off down the shaft we could hear the faint clanging of an alarm. We waited. He pushed the alarm button again and kept it clangling, just in the hope that some gnome in the basement might recognize our distress signal as a call to duty.

An empty elevator offers very little in the way of entertainment. The minutes dragged on. Finally a distant voice shouted, "What floors are you between?" "Nine and ten," George screamed back, and our spirits rose. A few minutes later the motor begun to hum, and down we went to the lobby, feeling as though we had been sprung from an illegal jail term. The exhilaration of our freedom—not only from the elevator, but from the curse of the day as well—turned the rest of the day into a special holiday. We splurged on dinner at the Ritz—that elegant bastion of civilized society where waiters and elevators move sliently and smoothly on their appointed rounds.

"And Ships"

None of my ancestors came over on the Mayflower. But one of my father's did squeeze onto her sister ship the Speedwell, which was also named after a flower more commonly known as Veronica. The Speedwell started out on that famous 1620 voyage with the Mayflower, but she proved unseaworthy and her expedition was delayed. Both ships must have been riding low in the water, if all the ancestors who are claimed as passengers were really on board. And when you see the replica of the Mayflower, it seems incredible that 102 people could have been jammed into that small hull for two months. Not my idea of a pleasure cruise. Can you imagine the living conditions?

Claiming descent from a passenger on either ship has never been very important to me, but it was to my mother. Her own family were Johnnies-come-lately who didn't cross the Atlantic until the 1850s. She was enamored of genealogy, and when she couldn't find attractive fruit on her own family tree, she was delighted to pluck this plum from my father's and bestow it on her daughters and granddaughters.

The fact is that I know very little about ships. Both of my parents grew up in the Midwest, and my mother saw an ocean for the first time when she was twenty-seven years old. She saw a lot of it for the next eight weeks, while she and my father sailed from San Fransisco to Japan. She was a good sailor and won prizes for shuffleboard and a very gentile form of deck tennis, played in long skirts and a huge hat anchored by veils and scarves. My poor father could get seasick in the bathtub. Crossing the channel from Calais to Dover gave him ample time to turn green and part with his lunch. But he was an inveterate traveler, and after twenty-four hours of misery he enjoyed every one of the many crossings—with the exception of the troopship crossing when he went to Italy in 1918. He never spoke of that, and when he returned from the war, I saw him cry for the first time. It made quite an impression on my four-year-old mind. I didn't know fathers or mothers cried.

My sister's first voyage was a long one, too. She was nine months old when my parents returned from two years in Argentina. It took twenty-one days to sail from Buenos Aires to New York, and the ship's carpenter built a little wooden crib into a bunk. That was four years before I was born, so I don't remember it too well. But when I was seven, my parents, my maternal grandparents, my sister, and I sailed on the Olympic to Cherbourg for a year in Switzerland. I remember that trip very well. The fog horn terrified me, and I kept my fingers in my ears all one foggy day. On the sunny days a small boy and I devoted every waking moment to picking up discarded cigarette butts, removing the scraps of tobacco, filling an empty pipe tin with our loot, and then proudly presenting it to his pipe-smoking father. It never occurred to us that he wouldn't be thrilled with our gift. He must have been a kind man; I remember only that he assured us that he wouldn't need any more for the rest of the trip. When we docked I was surprised to see porters wearing smocks and berets, and they weren't black, like the porters I had encountered before.

I remember taking the boat from Geneva up the lake to Vevey or Montreux. It was May and the pink horse chestnut trees that lined the quais were in bloom. Mont Blanc made a brief, spectacular appearance, and at the other end of the lake, the Dent du Midi was equally impressive. "A host of golden daffodils" raced down the hillsides of Montreux, pleasing an eight-year-old more than the dank dungeons of Chillon.

When I was eleven, we spent part of the summer at a small lake in northern New Jersey. The owner of our cottage had built a beautiful little rowboat, hardly seven feet long, painted red. It was light and responsive to the least dip of its small oars, and it became my sole domain for a month. No one cautioned me to be careful. I knew how lovingly Mr. Scranton had made the boat, and I would have scraped my knees sooner than its hull. I explored every inch of that lake from the reedy end, where I could hide among the cattails and red-wing blackbirds' nests, to the rocky cliffs at the north end. I saw blue herons, a wary muskrat, and buzzards circling high in the sky. No captain of the Queen Elizabeth II ever felt more in command of his vessel.

There have been other boats in my life—canoes in Maine and on Lac des Isles in Quebec. We stayed on a tiny island, and our only means of transportation was our canoe. How hard it must have been for my mother, who couldn't swim and feared the water, to sit on the bottom of the canoe, exactly in the middle, with her legs straight out and her white knuckles clutching the gunwales.

I've only sailed a few times in South Bristol, Maine, in Elbert Manchester's sailboat. One day in August we got becalmed and the rise and fall of the ground swells brought on what I hope will be my only case of sea sickness. George and I have sailed with Sam and Jane Rowley out of New London, Connecticut, to Fisher's Island. Long Island Sound outdid itself in working up a tremedous storm. We bobbed around like a cork soaked by the wash. Only Sam's skill kept us from capsizing.

Steven Page, our son-in-law, is not only a true sailor but a builder of wooden boats as well. We had one brief, bumpy sail on Lake Champlain with him and Debbie and one-year-old Morgan. Morgan went to sleep in a small bunk in the bow of the cabin. As long as the waves slapped and whammed against the hull, he slept peacefully. When we got back to the calm water at the mooring, he woke up and protested loudly. He must have his father's nautical genes to have been rocked in the cradle of the deep that day.

The slowest boat I've ever been on was a punt on the Char in Oxford. My first attempt at punting convinced me that it is an acquired English skill like cricket. Both look like sleep-walking but turn out to be very difficult for an American to master. You have to shove the pole down into the bottom of the shallow river and give a vigorous heave. The punt moves smoothly along, but the pole stays imbedded in the mud and you are stretched ominously between the two. If you let go of the pole, there you are up the river without an oar. If you don't let go, you are soon in the drink minus your dignity. How can it look so easy?

The fastest ship in my limited experience was the flygbot from Copenhagen to Malmo, Sweden. It looks like a benign enough little launch, but shortly after take off the motor revs up and you are airborne literally riding above the waves at high speed. When we were in Copenhagen visiting Patty's family, we stayed at the Admiral Hotel, a reconstructed warehouse right alongside the docks. Nothing but a promenade separates the thick stone walls of the hotel from Ore Sund, the sound of the Baltic Sea. The great, white liners to Bornholm and Oslo slipped in and out silently. At bedtime we would be looking right onto the lighted deck of the Prinz Olaf, and in the morning the ship alongside would be the Margrethe. No blasts of the fog horn, no chugging of engines, or shouts from the sailors. Just huge, silent, white ships that passed in the night.

The most ghostly ship was a big, dark, Russian fishing trawler that was forced to drop anchor in our cove on the coast of Maine one foggy night. The fog was so dense that we didn't hear or see her until the dark hull loomed up a few hundred feet of shore. Several of us teenagers jumped into a dory and rowed out. It was a dirty-looking boat, manned by a bearded crew. They threw a rope ladder over the side and we climbed aboard. The men in dark turtlenecks stood around awkwardly, shy and speechless, staring at the deck. One of them spoke a little English and told us they had been at sea for three months and it would be another month before they returned home. This was in the '30s before we had been brainwashed about the Russians, and we felt sorry for these homesick sailors. In the morning the fog had lifted and they were gone. Was it a phantom ship?

Twenty years later, we were living in South Burlington when the side-wheeler Ticonderoga was moved overland to its present dry dock at the Shelburne Museum. A strange apparition, with smoke stacks and decks poking up above the pine trees, as they inched and winched it along on railroad tracks. It was undignified somehow for that graceful ship to be so helpless on land, like a swan waddling awkwardly to its nest. We had sailed many times on the Ti, but I remember one night in particular—all the lights on board were blazing and the huge, shining pistons were thrusting up and down. As we neared the dock, the flaming coals were shovelled into the water, a pyrotechnic display better than fireworks. At the museum she has been beautifully restored, and thousands of tourists walk her decks every summer. But her engines are silent, and there is no slap of waves against her hull.

"Of Shoes"

I got shoes. You got shoes.
All God's chillun got shoes.
When I get to heaven, goin' t' put on my shoes
And goin' to walk all over God's heaven.

From the time the first cave man got fed up with pulling thorns out of his feet and tied a piece of deerskin around his sore foot with a leather thong, shoes have been status symbols as well as protective covering. In Europe, I have been told, people tell Americans by their shoes. European shoes do look different, though it is hard to say just why—a little broader perhaps and with thicker soles. Venetian ladies, in the Renaissance period, walked around on raised shoes that were almost stilts. The shoes not only elevated them above the common folk but also kept their feet above the flotsam and jetsam that littered the cobbled streets.

A modern young woman admires high heels because they add to her height and make her feel feminine and attractive. Although comfort and protection may have been the original motivations, shoe fashions have done much to enrich podiatrists. Corns and bunions are the penalty for wearing shoes that are too small, and the salesgirl who moans, "Oh my feet are killing me," wouldn't be caught dead behind the counter in arch preservers.

Country and Western singers whose phosphorescent jeans have never met saddle leather invest as much in their tooled and jeweled boots as in their guitars. Cowboy boots also have heels which make the wearer taller without detracting from his macho image.

Buying the first pair of high heels is a rite of passage from childhood to the doubtful pleasures of adolescence. I remember the long years when my sensible mother kept postponing the great day and the humiliation in third grade of having to wear high shoes to school when some of my classmates had graduated to oxfords. Until you reach the age of reason, whatever you wear has to be a clone of your peers' clothing. That was true for saddle shoes, penny loafers, and now Addidas. The mother of a second grader told me she had to pay a good deal more for her daughter's running shoes than her husband had paid for his size eleven loafers.

The first Mrs. Nelson Rockefeller caused quite a stir at a reception in Albany when her husband was governor by taking off her shoes because she felt she was towering above the guests. It doesn't seem to worry Susan Anton or Nancy Kissinger to be taller than Dudley Moore or Henry Kissinger, but then neither of those gentlemen lacks for attention in his own right.

Probably the most extreme example of the status of shoes is tiny embroidered, pointed slippers worn by the aristocratic Chinese ladies who had had their feet bound when they were children. I have a pair of them that my mother brought back from China in 1907. They are only five inches long with red silk embroidered sides and pale blue quilted soles that never touched pavement. They didn't touch floors a great deal either because hobbling around was painful. But the mincing walk was considered feminine and aristocratic. Big (natural) feet were only for peasants and western women, who also had big noses and eyes and therefore were ugly. Small feet are still esteemed in our culture, even though the average woman's foot size has grown from a six and a half to an eight and a half in the last twenty years, and Jackie Kennedy Onassis wears a size ten. Part of the popularity of high-heeled shoes is that they make a woman's feet look shorter. Sometimes the length of feet has been camouflaged by long, upturned toes on the court jester's footgear or red Turkish slippers.

There are examples where practicality won out over vanity. The Dutch wooden shoes keep feet dry in the lowlands. Racing sled dogs wear little, leather booties to protect their paws from the constant abrasion of running on snow and rough ice. Fishermen wear waders so they can be partly submerged in trout streams, and the lobstermen on the coast of Maine wear hip boots with the tops turned down like firemen's boots. The purpose in both cases is to keep feet dry, but I often wondered about the practicality of the lobstermen's hip boots, when every year some poor lobsterman while leaning over the side of his boat to haul in a lobster trap loses his balance in the rough sea and topples overboard. The hip boots instantly fill with water and drag him down. Sadly enough, few lobstermen know how to swim. What's the point when the boots would pull him down anyway?

In some countries shoes stay outdoors or just on the warm side of the door where they are removed upon entering. In Japan, the clogs used to be parked inside the door, and you put on those little, one-toed socks and raffia sandals as you came in. It kept the house clean and quiet. Every time I remove a large clod of mud or less desirable substances from the carpet, I yearn for the wisdom of the East. Shoes are taboo in mosques, also. In Finland, where the winters are long, dark, and wet, it is a common rite to remove your shoes just inside the door of a private home. Our little Finnish-American grandsons cast their shoes automatically when they come into our house, even though their visits have always been in the summer.

Baby shoes are so wrapped in nostalgia that you find them hanging from car mirrors, like an amulet, or given a place of honor on a bookself. I have to admit that well-worn baby shoes are endearing. Little three-year-old Morgan has a row of tiny boots, red felt ones worn by his cousins in Finland, yellow rubber ones, snow mobile boots, and minute, chunky, jogging shoes that make me laugh out loud at their miniature, macho image. When Debbie, his mother, was two, she used to shed her sneakers twenty times a day and then cradle her left foot, while she sniffed the inside of her right elbow and sucked her right thumb. She is still limber, though she gave up that particular contortion before she went to school. Every summer she lost at least one small sneaker in the hay loft. It was always found the next spring when Ralph Nealy was pitching down the last of the hay. Of course by then the sneaker had been outgrown and its useless mate long discarded.

Which reminds me that Debbie is one of the few brides to wear sneakers to her wedding. The wedding was outdoors, down at the brook, in the rain. Debbie had made her long white gown and was determined to wear it, but hated to drown her new shoes in the mud. So when her father, shod in rubber boots, protected her from the worst of the deluge with a large black umbrella, Debbie marched down the bridal path in my well-worn, off-white tennis shoes. The guests, who were booted and raincoated, were too busy shivering and laughing to notice.

English usage is heavily shod. You can shake in your boots, die with your boots on, throw old shoes at the bride for luck, and wait for the other shoe to drop. Shoes have magic powers. Cinderella owed her emancipation and happiness to the fit of her glass slipper. Dorothy in *The Wizard of Oz* owed her power to the magic, ruby shoes coveted by the Wicked Witch of the West. I heard a small boy in a pediatricians's office ask wistfully, after he had been undressed, "Can I hold my shoes?" In a moment of stress they were his assurance of personhood. We may not all take comfort in our shoes or have seven league boots, but if we want a better world, we must learn what it feels like to walk in someone else's shoes.

Trees

Joyce Kilmer should have looked longer. I know some poems that are lovelier than some trees, as well as trees that are lovelier than a good deal of contemporary poetry. Think of all the trees that have shaded you literarily from Longfellow's spreading chestnut to the apple tree that you weren't supposed to sit under till he came marching home. When I was in fourth grade, we reluctantly memorized a poem, most of which I've long forgotten but the last lines were "on the top of the hill where all might see, God planted a scarlet maple tree." I never see a scarlet maple in October without silently saying those words. I can't see a cloud of white blossoms caught in a cherry tree in May without thinking of Housman's "Loveliest of trees, the cherry now is hung with bloom along the bough." Trees can be planted in the mind as well as the ground, and they never wither. Too bad that children don't memorize poetry now. Of course I hated it as a child. I stood sweaty-palmed in fear of forgetting a line in the middle of a recitation, but now I have reached the age when peripheral memory keeps Abou Ben Adhem on the tip of my tongue, while the number of my checking account plays will-o-the-wisp. My musician, ballerina, poet, choir-director friend Ellen Hensel can "say" poetry, as Robert Frost describes his readings, for an hour or more. It's a marvelous gift which must be a constant comfort to her as well as a great pleasure to her listeners. I have watched a group of women listening to one of her programs, and when she speaks through Emily Dickinson or through Sara Teasdale, for example, you can see that the thoughts of her audience are far away, reliving some long ago loss or a never entirely forgotten love.

The real trees in our lives, as well as those in literature, stay alive in memory. The most important tree in my early life was the big, old, sweet cherry tree in our backyard. It supported my swing when I was very small, and my treehouse, my secret place of refuge, when I was a little older. I can still smell its shiny, mahogany bark and feel the imprint of its branches on the soles of my sneakered feet. It was a friend for all seasons—a mass of fragrant, white flowers in April; then bright with cherries, first scarlet then wine-red, in May; a chorus of marauding robins in June; and a source of cool dark shade in mid-July.

I never drive west through South Burlington on I-89 past the house on Hinesburg Road where our children grew up without mourning the Northern Spy trees that were uprooted by bulldozers when they built the interstate. I remember careening across the field in our red truck and standing in the back of it under those trees reaching up to pick the red-streaked fruit, as precious to me as the golden apples of the Hesperides.

I remember another victim of the interstate, the shagbark hickory that always looked as though it was molting. Nothing is more frustrating than trying to blast the nut meats out of

those stone-hard, convoluted shells. It was the sort of job our girls called "milking a mouse," picky work for a miniscule result.

Then there were, or still are, unfortunately, those 8,000 white pine trees we planted twenty-four years ago here in Jericho. We did it under the guidance of the state forester and were promised fenceposts in twelve years, pulpwood in fifteen, and a tall stand of pines in twenty. Misshapen by blight, they are now useless and have cut off our view of the brook and the mountains. They do make cover for birds and wildlife which entertain us in winter, but they are not my favorite trees. Anything that stands there pointing an accusing finger at me for a past mistake does not warm my cockles. We can't even hire anyone to come in and cut several hundred of them. A pox on those pines! But there is, or was, an unusual elm down at the brook. It is unusual because it was seven trees in one. But with recent winter storms, it has been crashing down trunk by trunk. At the base there appeared to be one trunk, but hardly a foot above the ground it divided into seven large trunks that grew straight up together before sweeping out in the usual wineglass elm pattern. I admired that tree in its prime, and as it has begun to rot, birds and squirrels have liked it too and have built condominiums in its hollows. The only pileated woodpecker that I have ever seen on our land was in that tree, and I shall never forget how he and I stared at each other in disbelief. I'm sure we were both thinking, "How unbirdlike that creature is!"

When we visit our friends Jane and Sam Rowley on their lovely, former-plantation-land in Green Cove Springs, Florida, I marvel at the enormous live-oak trees that spread out over their house and lawns. And after a rain, the resurrection ferns

118

that grow along the mossy, horizontal limbs burst into brillant green. It is fun for a Vermonter to pick and eat a Satsuma orange or a persimmon from their trees, but I am a little in awe of the aged cyprus trees that stand with wet feet and knees in the St. John's River in their front yard. They have been told that they may be 900 years old, which means they were there when William the Conqueror invaded England. And they presided over those shores before the Spanish explorers came up the river. Any living thing that old deserves my respect.

I don't get chummy with a Saguaro or other cacti in the southwest. I like a tree to spread or reach, not to assume angular positions and prick my fingers. When we lived in Kansas, I never cared for the thorny Osage orange trees littering the streets with their large useless fruit. But I know that in the early years of settlement in Kansas, they were a help in holding water and in crowding together to make living fences to keep cattle in or out.

One always feels more at home with familiar living things whose habits we can anticipate. Because I grew up in the east, went to college in Massachusetts, and live in Vermont by choice, my favorites are Vermont trees, from the ubiquitous, pale-trunked "popple," to the glory of a golden tree tunnel of sugar maples. My first delights in spring are the gentle explosions of the pink-white shadbush blossoms throughout the woods. In midsummer the pines and cedars are redolent in the sun and offer cool, whispering shade in their depths. In fall there is the rampant conflagration of crimson swamp maples, apricot sugar maples, saffron beeches and wine-red oaks framed by the dark evergreens. And then in winter, the white farmhouses, red barns, and evergreens in their frosting of snow are animated Christmas cards.

When George was in Iran, he was depressed by the treeless mountains, by the almost total absence of green. When we lived in Kansas, I missed the forested hills of New England. I don't need the lush tropical verdure of Hawaii or the rain forest of Puerto Rico, but I am grateful that I live in Vermont where the mountains as well as the valleys are green.

A Season
of Color and Contrast

The first snowfall hints at the contrast in color that will follow. In early October you may wake to find snow on the mountains when the trees are still in full color in the valleys. And there is no sharper contrast than emerald-green spikes of grass poking through a light dusting of snow on the pastures. But later, when every field and wooded hillside is softened and deep with snow and stays that way for four months, the range of color in a white landscape is still very surprising.

If your inward eye pictures winter in Vermont in muted greys and browns, it isn't winter you are recalling. It is either November just before the snow covers the stubble on the khaki-colored corn fields, or mud season in late March when all the debris of winter—the fallen branches, lost scarf, broken exhaust pipes, and dog bones—surface for the first time since Thanksgiving.

The days are short, but for most of us, unless we are dairy farmers up at 5 A.M. year round, the shorter day means that we see both sunrise and sunset. Rosy-fingered dawn is not just a literary cliche. The siding on white farmhouses, white, steepled churches and eastern slopes are washed with a deli-

121

cate pink you remember from the inside of the conch shell on you grandmother's what-not. If you are lucky enough to catch sight of the eastern face of a now-covered mountain such as Mt. Mansfield or Camel's Hump, the entire top of the mountain is peach-blossom pink.

In case you sleep through sunrise, you are granted a second performance, on the western side of the mountains in the afternoon. This time all the white surfaces are tinted pale-gold. Long thundercloud-blue and mauve shadows stretch across the fields on one side of the house, but the west-facing side is lemon-yellow. Citrus colors are typical of winter sunsets, pastel-orange, yellow, and even green, contrast with the purple of the Adirondacks on the horizon. Sometimes the western sky glows with crimson fading to lavender, but there is always warm color in the west. Overhead, the winter sky is bright blue. Blackberry canes have the frosted, purple bloom of grapes, and the red osier twigs at the roadsides glow brighter against the snow.

A flock of pine grosbeaks, barely noticeable on a bare gravel road, are clearly visible now, and the rose-colored heads and breasts of the males are stained a deeper pink. Why are they always in the roads in the winter? Is it for salt or gravel? A sensible grosbeak should be cracking the cedar and beech seeds that he favors. That's what his big, strong beak was programmed for, and it is what his name *enucleator* means. We don't have cedar and beech trees near us, but why don't the birds enjoy the sunflower seed that we generously provide for their greedy cousins the evening grosbeaks?

We get a lot of flashing color at our feeders. If our ubiquitous bluejays were uncommon, imagine what our excitement would be at spotting one at the feeder! Only in winter do I fully appreciate the range of shades of blue in their

122

plumage once again, because of the contrast between their blues and the white snow and the yellow and black of the evening grosbeaks.

Red barns glow redder against the white snow. The gold-washed white houses stand out against the blue-shadowed fields.

Contrast is what makes winter special in Vermont. A warm house is unremarkable in summer. But the fragrant warmth when you stamp into a warm house in below zero weather! The sunlight seems twice as bright after two days of snow-filled skies. We blink like owls and complain happily about the glare to the gas station man or the check-out girl at the supermarket. Just getting to the barn without falling down is a victory over an unforgiving adversary. Bringing in wood is endless and hard work. Getting stuffed into jacket, cap, boots, and gloves and then unpeeling the whole soggy mess takes up a large portion of the day. The fact is that survival in the north country is a full-time occupation if you live close to the soil. This means heating partly with wood and, in some cases, keeping animals. But there is a sense of accomplishment when the chickens, geese, pigs, and sheep are fed, the wood is stacked, and the house is redolent of split-pea soup. I never experienced that living in an apartment. You shovel out the driveway and get the car started when it sounds like it would rather be left alone to sleep out the rest of the winter in the garage.

Winter is a challenge, a battle just to stay warm and fed. But as you mush out to the barn to collect the eggs for the fourth time in one day (they freeze if you don't), the whole western sky is pulsing with color. The geese bow and greet you formally, the hens murmur drowsily, and the pigs are aquiver with eager anticipation. Of course you could feel warmth on a beach in Florida and present a far more chic appearance on 5th Avenue. But here in Vermont we are semi-selfsufficient. There is purpose and satisfaction in our days, a sense of productivity and nurturing, even if it is as much our own spirit as well as the animals and land entrusted to our care.

The Christmas Letter

I always look foward to hearing from our old and distant friends at Christmas. I like to hear about their walks on the Great Wall of China and what their children are doing, but we always have at least one friend or relative who goes overboard and produces two or three single-spaced pages of Madison Avenue hype that is unbelievable. Just before Christmas last year we were having dinner with Dorcas and Charles Houston, and to my delight Charlie suggested that it was time to fight back verbally. I went home and wrote a tongue-in-cheek Christmas letter. He apparently did the same. We never mailed our satiric missives to the people on our Christmas card lists. But should the pen of one of your relatives prove as painful as a sword in describing the family that he sees only through rose-colored, magnifying glasses, calm down and read my un-mailed Christmas letter:

Dear - - - - ,
    Sleigh bells ring. Are you listening? You'd better because we've read your Christmas letters year after year after year. And this jolly season we want to share with you all the ful-

125

filling moments that have made this year memorable for us, the happy events and awards that have been bestowed on our little family.

George has once more been granted a sanitary landfill permit, and our membership in the National Geographic Society has been renewed for another year. I had no cavities at my last dental check-up. Neither did George, but that was hardly a surprise because he has the kind of teeth that are guaranteed not to develop cavities.

Sitting here in front of the fire, invisible since we converted to a woodstove, which just emitted a puff of smoke destined to set off the smoke alarm, which makes the dog howl and wakes the grandchild who was taking his only nap in weeks, I think back over the past year and wish that I hadn't.

Although retired, George has the same teaching assignments he had before but with one small difference. He no longer gets paid for them. But he finds it rewarding to work at two other part time jobs, which pay just too much for him to be eligible for his full social security benefits. He also continues his seasonal brave struggles with the thirty-year-old rototiller that tips over in the garden, ingesting mud in its vital parts. Maggie joined him in the garden to hunt for a lost bolt, creeping along with a magnet, which ignored the bolt, but attracted several stones. We had not been previously aware that our annual crop of rocks was ferrous. His other adversaries are the lawn mover that starts at will—its will not George's—and the snowblower that throws large pieces of gravel onto what we laughingly refer to as our lawn.

Patty and Tage and their boys moved from Helsinki to Copenhagen where Patrick promptly got lost in the Tivoli Gardens. Peter swallowed a Danish coin which has never been retrieved, and Patty dropped a plank on her foot on moving day. While they were redecorating their new house, Peter spilled a full can of blue paint, Patrick threw a ball through a window, and their furniture was about to be impounded until the required papers were signed. They love the friendliness of Denmark, but I won't bore you with that sort of news.

Debbie has a new teaching job which she likes, but two weeks after school started, she landed in the hospital for a lung operation which left her in intense pain for the first three weeks and limp as a rag for the rest of the fall. Towards the end of this interlude, their baby Morgan threw up all over Steve and passed on his GI infection to his adoring father.

Maggie sold fifteen pumpkins to Desso's store in October and set off the burglar alarm by mistake. She spends most of her time wandering around the house trying to find a chair that doesn't produce low back pain. She snores so loudly that George got bored with her bed and sleeps upstairs. Well not real sleep. It's an unreasonable facsimile, because he wakes up at 4 A.M. and frets over such things as nuclear war and why the rats, which infested the barn last winter, have deserted the premises. Do they know something we don't know?

So once again we wish you and your children, who get straight A's and early admission to Havard with full scholarships, and your husband, who was voted Business Man of the Year in Skokie and ran successfully for dog catcher, and his charming wife, who got her law degree summa cam laude, after eight years of night school and has just been appointed the second women on the Supreme Court, the joys of the season.

If our wishes for you come true, your Christmas tree will fall over on Grandmother, you will have a power failure when the turkey is half done, and flame proof brandy with which to annoint you Christmas pudding. May all the children's games

127

come without batteries and your bonus check get burned up with the wrappings. And perhaps this conflagration may result in a chimney fire, bringing the volunteer fire department to your hearth to sit around, dripping in their boots, sampling your Christmas spirits, and selling you tickets to the Firemen's Ball.

With love from,

Maggie and George,
two pigs, 24 laying hens,
two sheep, four turkeys
and a partridge in a pine tree

Sounds of Winter

"It's so quiet here," our city friends say when they visit us in winter. You sense a certain ambivalence. They are soothed by the silence, but they also miss the sounds that symbolize familiar activities to them. Winter in Vermont is neither silent nor inactive. Some sounds are muffled. Our brook which roars in March and talks in a conversational tone in summer is in a state of partial hibernation. The pool is frozen and snow-covered except for a dark pupil in its oval white eye where the water is still sliding over the waterfall to swirl for a moment in the open space before moving silently down stream under its tent of ice.

Falling snow muffles and distorts the sound of voices and takes a little of the abrasive edge off the whine of a chain saw or the imperative roar of a snowmobile. Why must snow-mobiles be so noisy? Certainly someone could invent a better muffler. I suspect that snowmobilers LIKE the sound. Un-fortunately, the lovely, deep silence of the woods in winter is sometimes sliced open by a chain saw (which at least serves a useful purpose) and the snowmobile (which symbolizes to me only an atavistic urge to feel dominant by going faster and making more noise and being more thoughtless than other people).

There are many, small, pleasant sounds that ornament rather

than break the winter silence. The whir of a chickadee's wings almost touching my hair when I fill the feeder. The plop of a huge marshmallow of snow slipping off a pine tree. The distant but oncoming rattle and scrape of the snowplow—a cheerful reminder that although we don't have to go out, we could if we wanted to. We are not snowbound unless we want to use it as an excuse. Our snowblower is George's foul-weather friend and delight. It starts cheerfully in contrast to most of the lawnmowers and garden tillers we've had.

As I walk out for the mail, I can almost tell the temperature by the sound of my footsteps. If it is above zero, my steps produce a series of crunches or soft footfalls, depending on the texture of the snow. But when the temperature sinks well below zero, each footstep makes a high-pitched squeak.

Our pool is not deep enough for us to hear the booming and groaning of ice forming that scares or regales our friends who live on the lake. And I don't spend enough time down there in the winter at night to hear it if it did complain. But up in the house late at night there are sharp retorts in the roof. Old Vermonters say "the nails are popping," but none seem to pop out or even show their heads, and no boards or beams are split. No wonder the eskimos endowed their climate with spirits. Our upstairs ceilings and roof, inanimate most of the year, stage some sort of invisible but noisy Fourth of July-in-January celebration.

Nothing seems to fall apart as a result of these revels, but there are some winter sounds that bode no good—like the ping and rattle of sleet which threatens to ice over our road. It rarely happens, but there is no more helpless feeling than driving a car which slews and dances to the beat of a different drummer. Another sad winter sound is the spinning of tires. There is a curve on the hill just past our driveway, and every winter several drivers underestimate their speed and over-

130

estimate their traction with the result that they skid and thump into the ditch. First you hear the thump, then a period of silence, then the spinning of tires, then the car door slams, and shortly there is a knock on the door. They always hope that we have a tractor and chains or a vehicle heavy enough to pull them out. We don't, so the best we can do is let them use our phone to ask husband, father, or garageman to rescue them.

We only hear one end of the conversation, but from the long silences and wistful words, it is easy to deduce that the person on the other end is less than fascinated by the news. One young girl, who had just flipped a Jeep completely over and should have been rejoicing that she was unhurt, arrived moaning, "My husband is going to kill me! He'll just kill me." He didn't, but one father flatly refused to get dressed (this usually happens at night) and come to the aid of his teen-age daugther. He apparently suggested that she walk home, three miles on a slippery road at night in the pelting rain. She refused our help and set off bravely, saying that someone would probably pick her up. I hope a nice someone did.

Sometimes the car will crash through our fence and gouge deep tracks in the yard. Two young boys did this and begged us not to tell their parents. They promised they would come back the next day after school to mend it. We didn't and they did, with one of them working on it until after dark. The only trouble is that after multiple contusions and amateur repair jobs, our fence is standing mostly through habit.

But on a winter day when the snow sifts down steadily rounding out and softening the contours of the meadows and the pine trees are soughing softly, the sounds of winter are as soporific as a lullaby and as comforting as a mother's good-night kiss.

Winter in Vermont

Winter in Vermont is trial by wood, fire and ice, snow, and intense cold. When a fifth generation Vermonter says, "If I make it through the winter," he is simply stating a fact of life, a matter of survival dependent on activity. There are sub-zero days when standing still could result in permanent immobility. So you don't stand still. When someone "from away" asked a self-sufficient octogenarian what she did in the winter, she snapped," If you had to feed two wood stoves for six months you wouldn't ask such a fool question!"

But it is equally obvious that Vermont in winter is an animated Christmas card. The white farmhouses and steepled churches are washed with pale-gold light in the afternoon, contrasting harmoniously with the long blue shadows on the snow. Red barns look much more scenic in winter when their roofs wear a thick mantle of snow. Of course the heavy burden tests the endurance of barn or porch roof supports. It also tests the back and balance of the shoveler who struggles up on the roof to relieve some of the overload. Snow is heavy stuff. One of the kindest inventions for north country dwellers is the snowblower. A driveway is cleared in minutes instead of hours.

Snow is not only for shovelling. A steep hillside becomes a sliding hill and echoes with the shouts of children who trudge silently uphill and shriek all the way down. Snow is for a horse to roll in, refreshing and scratching his barn-dusty back. And snow is for children to collapse in and make angel wings, relaxing for a moment in its soft depth and looking up into a buttermilk sky.

Trial by ice is the resistance of the frozen water to an ice saw. It is a test of skill on skates and staying upright when you are the tail end of crack-the-whip.

Winter is a tightrope act, remaining vertical on a sleety road, keeping your car out of the ditch, and hoarding heat in your house, your hands, and your toes.

But how can you appreciate "the electric," until you experience the wonderful surge of light and power after an outage? And how can you know the benison of warmth, unless your face is stiff with cold, and your fingers and toes are protesting painfully?

You have to lose something for a while to fully appreciate it, whether it be a love or a season. Could your heart leap at the sight of a crocus or robin if they were with you all year? And even in winter in Vermont, your underlying faith and the buds that are already formed on the trees tell you that, after the cold and the dark, the days will lengthen, the sun will have more warmth, and the sap in the sugar maples will rise once more to lift your spirit with its sweet promise of spring.